Praise for *Green Careers*:
You Can Make Money AND Save the Planet

"An encouraging portrait of a can-do generation."
– *Publishers Weekly*

"[Scott] makes clear in this lively overview that lucrative, soul-satisfying environmental careers are not 'some far-fetched green dream' ... Informative and inspiring for teens, this may also draw adults seeking new career directions." – *Booklist*

"The emphasis put on 'green jobs' by President Obama and the global recognition of environmental responsibility are already resulting in a whole new employment sector. This is why *Green Careers* is a well-timed and useful guide for high school and college students ... Each of the people profiled is youthful, vibrant and intriguing."
– *ForeWord*

"... there is no denying the breadth and variety of information provided here ... a worthwhile volume for aspiring planet-savers and money makers." – *Quill & Quire*

"... shines a spotlight on some potentially lucrative and stable choices that are available to the next generation of job-seekers ... This is a stellar resource ..." – *Resource Links*

To Jeff, Juliet, Sydney Rose, Mom, and Dad
— Jennifer Power Scott

Green Careers
You Can Make Money AND Save the Planet
Text © 2010 Jennifer Power Scott

Published by Lobster Press™
1620 Sherbrooke Street West, Suites C & D
Montréal, Québec H3H 1C9
Tel. (514) 904-1100 • Fax (514) 904-1101 • www.lobsterpress.com

Publisher: Alison Fripp
Editor: Meghan Nolan
Editorial Assistants: Mahak Jain & Nicole Watts
Proofreader: Katherine Mason
Indexer: Estalita Slivoskey
Production Manager: Tammy Desnoyers
Cover Design: Christian Fünfhausen
Design and Typesetting: Lynda Arthur

Canadian Heritage   Patrimoine canadien   We acknowledge the financial support of the Government of Canada through the Canada Book Fund for our publishing activities.

Melanie Mullen and Camille Labchuk were two of several young people featured in the author's article, "Green Warriors," in the April 2008 "Go Green Issue" of *Canadian Living* magazine. The author interviewed Melanie and Camille again and expanded their stories in this book. Both profiles feature quotes that originally appeared in the *Canadian Living* article.

The quote from Mark Vanderheyden of RWDI in Erica Stolp's profile originally appeared in the author's article, "Green Warriors," in the "Go Green Issue" of *Canadian Living* magazine in April 2008.

Library and Archives Canada Cataloguing in Publication

Power Scott, Jennifer, 1968-
        Green careers : you can make money and save the planet / Jennifer Power Scott.

ISBN 978-1-897550-18-2

        1. Environmental protection--Juvenile literature. 2. Environmental responsibility--Juvenile literature. 3. Environmental protection--Vocational guidance--Juvenile literature. I. Title.

GE195.5.P69 2010   j333.72   C2009-900036-9

Printed and bound in Canada using soy based inks and certified FSC paper.

GREEN
CAREER$
YOU CAN MAKE MONEY
– AND –
SAVE THE PLANET

JENNIFER POWER SCOTT

Lobster Press ™

Table of Contents

Acknowledgements

It happened on my birthday, if you can believe it. I sat at my computer to check my e-mail and found a message from Lobster Press. The editor was offering me the opportunity to write a book about environment-related careers. Becoming an author was my greatest career dream, so that e-mail was better than double-chocolate birthday cake with whipped cream, chunks of brownie, and assorted sparkly sprinkles.

I said yes, of course. And now, after more than a year of digging, contemplating, planning, interviewing, writing, and rewriting, a great idea has turned into a book.

And a very cool, colorful, busting-out-with-great-stories kind of book at that.

Here's where I get to thank the people who helped make *Green Careers* happen. First, there's Kathryn Dorrell, an editor at *Canadian Living* magazine. When the magazine was planning its "Go Green" issue for the spring of 2008, she asked me to write a story about young people in environmental careers. Lobster Press read the story, liked it, and decided to contact me with the book idea. So without you, Kathryn, this book would not exist.

I thank Alison Fripp, president and publisher of Lobster Press, for recognizing the *Canadian Living* article was the seed of something bigger. And I thank my editor, Meghan Nolan, for her unfaltering enthusiasm, patience, and dedication to the project. Meghan, I admire your creativity, command of the language, and attention to detail. Working with you has been a pleasure.

I also send green cheers to Erin Simnitt and Laura Benshoff, editorial assistants with Lobster Press, who did an amazing job digging up stats, websites, articles, and other great material. Your superb research made *Green Careers* a better book.

As I perused the planet for fantastic folks to interview, so many people helped in the search. Thanks to the Jane Goodall Institute (JGI), the National Oceanic and Atmospheric Administration (NOAA), Aga Khan Foundation Canada, the Whale and Dolphin Conservation Society (WDCS), the University of Waterloo, the Nova Scotia Community College, the University of Colorado at Boulder, the College of the Atlantic (COA), Sheridan College, Fanshawe College, principal Marijke Blok at Saint John High School, the Environmental Careers Organization (ECO Canada), Green For All, Great Ape Trust of Iowa, the American Institute of Architects (AIA), Bryant Terry, Starbucks, Deborah Lindquist, Jennifer Phillips of Red Light PR, Scientific Certification Systems (SCS), Rowan Williams Davies & Irwin Inc. (RWDI), the Canadian Association of Physicians for the Environment (CAPE), the Environmental Working Group (EWG), Caroline Lee, Alexander Gill, Bill Costigane, and the Chartered Institute of Environmental Health.

I thank all of the remarkable people I had the pleasure of interviewing for *Green Careers*. Your stories, which will take readers from the Arctic to Africa to Oregon, are inspiring, exciting, and moving. It was an honor getting to know you.

I thank my parents, Philip and Sheila Power of Grand Falls-Windsor, Newfoundland, for always making me believe I could achieve anything ... and for letting me boast ad nauseam about *Green Careers*!

ACKNOWLEDGEMENTS

I thank my startlingly handsome husband, Jeff Scott, a gifted high school teacher, theatre director, and musician. He kept me in touch with what's cool — and important — to today's teens. He also shot my publicity photographs. (The occasional hot breakfast delivered to my desk didn't hurt either.)

Thanks to Ashley Reynolds, who took such excellent care of my children while I wrote *Green Careers*. You are going to be a marvelous schoolteacher.

And finally, I thank my darling little girls, Juliet and Sydney Rose. Guys, this is what your mommy was doing in the home office all those months. Maybe someday these stories will inspire you too.

Yes. I think they will.

Introduction

> **It's a green revolution, really. Concern for the environment is making its way into all our lives and almost every profession. Companies need smart, talented, creative people – and lots of them – to keep up with all of that change. And you know what that means: Jobs.**

Want to help save the world and earn a paycheck at the same time?

OK, maybe that sounds like a joke, or some far-fetched green dream. But it's not. If you've grown up with a passion for the planet, an eye for all things environmental, and an unshakeable feeling that you have to do something – anything – for Mother Earth, I have good news for you. The environmental job market is booming ... big time. Not just in the United States and Canada, but all over the world. For people with the right skills, the green career choices are almost unlimited. There are jobs for conservation biologists. Jobs for wind turbine fabricators. Jobs for environmental engineers. Jobs for activists. Jobs for green business experts. Jobs for oceanographers. Jobs for air quality specialists. Jobs for meteorologists. Jobs for green fashion designers. Jobs for organic chefs. Jobs for ...

Whew! You get the picture.

Now here's even better news for you. Right now, at least, lots of great employers can't find enough fresh talent to fill those jobs. Companies all over the planet are thirsty for workers with environmental know-how. Even when economic times are tough, the environmental sector is, as engineer Robert Niven told me, "recession resistant." If you get yourself some eco-skills and savvy, chances are you will find work reasonably quickly. And if you have entrepreneurial spirit, you could always create your own environment-related business. In the 21st century, it's all about the big green job machine.

Why?

Well, mainly because the world finally figured out that we have to work together to fight climate change and protect the planet for ourselves, our children, and our grandchildren. Governments are forcing big industries to curb toxic emissions. Architects are designing buildings that last longer, work better, and cause less harm to the environment. Factories have to pass environmental impact studies before they're built. People are becoming more and more concerned about how toxins in our homes and communities are affecting our health. Organizations like Ducks Unlimited and the Jane Goodall Institute are working harder than ever to help endangered species and protect habitats. And families, maybe like yours, are demanding Earth-friendly products like biodegradable plastic bags, non-toxic cleaners, and organic foods.

It's a green revolution, really. Concern for the environment is making its way into all our lives and almost every profession. Companies need smart, talented, creative people — and lots of them — to keep up with all of that change. And you know what that means: Jobs.

It wasn't like this when your parents and grandparents were teenagers. There was an environmental movement, but it was on the fringes, not in people's faces. There wasn't all that much talk about global warming. Lots of people let the water run while they brushed their teeth. They threw everything into the trash, and they didn't worry a whole lot about what exactly was billowing out of factory smokestacks. Recycling was a new idea. And composting? Well, that was just one of those odd things hippies did in their backyards.

Yes, most people had some inkling there were environmental problems in the 1970s and '80s. A few stood up and tried to fight for change. But as Professor Jim White of the University of Colorado at Boulder told me, his generation missed the opportunity to step up and take this on.

The teens of the 21st century are different. Better, in some ways. You have grown up knowing the Earth isn't something to harm or take for granted. Recycling and composting are normal parts of your life. The lust for more and more stuff isn't necessarily your driving force. Maybe you're even the "green police" in your house, pushing your parents to switch off the lights, buy hybrid cars, and hang clothes in the

sun to dry. For many people your age, taking care of the planet is a whole lot more than just the cool thing to do. It's a passion, even the cause that helps define your generation.

Professor White, in fact, calls this the most interesting time on Earth since the discovery of fire. How's that for a big statement?

❝ Maybe you're even the "green police" in your house, pushing your parents to switch off the lights, buy hybrid cars, and hang clothes in the sun to dry. For many people your age, taking care of the planet is a whole lot more than just the cool thing to do. It's a passion, even the cause that helps define your generation. ❞

Green Careers is a book of many stories. Mind-blowing ones that will sometimes take your breath away, make you think, maybe even make you cry. You will meet more than 30 remarkable young people who are painting their careers in vibrant shades of green. They will take us around the world, from the icebergs of the Arctic Ocean, to a life-changing new power plant in the African jungle, to the eye of a hurricane. (Hold on for *that* ride!)

You'll get to know a guy who spends his life helping a family of apes, another who has built a business empire on worm poop and garbage, and another who is devoted to sharing the magic of nature with inner-city kids. We'll meet a young activist who ran for political office when she was barely old enough to vote, a Londoner whose environmental health career has him rubbing elbows (well, almost!) with the likes of Kylie Minogue, and a world-class pianist who performed at Carnegie Hall in a dress made of garbage. (It's prettier than it sounds.)

These green warriors will wow you. And that's a promise.

Of course, it's important to emphasize that you don't have to be an activist to have an environmental career. This was pointed out to me many times during

the research. Alexa Pagel, a young environmental worker you will meet in Chapter 4, told me people wrongly assume she's a "tree hugger" or "granola-eating hippie." Tom Szaky, one of the entrepreneurs featured in Chapter 1, is up front about the fact he's a capitalist, not an environmentalist. And Andrew Walsh, someone you'll meet in Chapter 8, gives environmental employment a whole different twist in his position as a safety advisor for the British Broadcasting Corporation (BBC). So, while many of the people in this book *are* impassioned activists, the green job market has room for everyone.

Green Careers is a series of self-contained profiles. That means it will make sense even if you choose not to read the book from beginning to end. Depending on what interests you, be it technical careers, nature, the artsy side of being green, or something else, you can jump from profile to profile. Most of the stories are written in a narrative style, but I have also added some short point-form profiles under the heading *A Budding Career*. These stories feature young people who are still in school, doing volunteer work, or getting started in green careers.

To make the book even more useful, there are also loads of sidebars full of amazing facts on topics like trash, green roofs, cool environmental websites, eco-tourism, and even eco-bikinis! And there are "Spotlight" features about universities, colleges, and professors.

And finally, be sure to check out the "Resources" section for details on everything from environmental schools to cool green websites.

I have loved meeting and writing about the people in this book, and I know you will enjoy reading their stories. I am not exaggerating when I say they have left me impressed, sometimes astonished, and so very excited about the future. For all the problems we face, this is a great place in history, a time of change and hope. And the career opportunities out there are as vast as the Atlantic, as high as the ozone, as lush as the boreal forest.

Whether you choose an environmental career or something else you love, good luck finding your way.

Chapter 1

ECO
ENTREPRENEURS

The Million-Dollar Garbage Man

TOM SZAKY, CEO, TerraCycle

Do you think it's possible to build a $35-million empire on worm poop and garbage?

Tom Szaky believed it could happen. Yes, he was convinced his stinky, sticky idea could spell big-time dollars. He was committed to it. He didn't give up. And now, at the age of 26, the guy with the boyish grin and spiky brown hair is founder and CEO of TerraCycle, Inc., one of the hottest, most exciting eco-businesses in North America.

> **❝ ... a college dropout who makes a living collecting trash, doing cool things with trash ... and talking trash. ❞**

Tom has 65 people working for him in two countries. He gives lectures and interviews all over the planet. The Harvard Business School invited him to speak. *Inc.* magazine even made him a cover boy (dressed in his trademark t-shirt and jeans) and called TerraCycle "the coolest little start-up in America."[1] All this for a college dropout who makes a living collecting trash, doing cool things with trash ... and talking trash.

So what's the secret of this garbage king's smelly success?

"Hard work," says Tom, fresh from a breakfast meeting where another investor agreed to throw a big chunk of money into TerraCycle. "Believing in a dream and then going after it. And working really hard to accomplish it. I think, especially in North America, if you work really hard, you can pull it off."

Let's step back a few years and find out how Tom's amazing story began. He and his family moved from Hungary to Toronto, Canada, as refugees when he was about six years old. He says he enjoyed living in Canada, and he grew up seeing North America as a place where you can achieve any goal if you try hard enough. When he was 14, he showed off his budding entrepreneurial zest by setting up his own web design company. A few years later, he got on a plane and went to New Jersey to study behavioral economics at the ultra-prestigious Princeton University.

But it was a trip to Montreal that changed Tom's life. His friends were growing stubborn plants in their basement. "They were having a really hard time with it," Tom says. "And when they started feeding worm poop to their plants, that's when everything started going really well. What I got inspired by was the fact that they were taking garbage and feeding it to the worms and then creating a really cool product. That's what got me really excited."

Tom couldn't forget that product: the potent little poop. And when the Princeton Entrepreneurship Club announced it was

COMPUTERS IN BLOOM

What do old computers have to do with plants? The Urban Art Pot, that's what. It's an 8-inch flower pot made of 100 percent "e-waste." TerraCycle came up with the idea of turning tossed-out fax machines and computers into planters. On top of being functional, the US$8.99 Urban Art Pot is super stylish. Graffiti artists paint each one by hand in psychedelic blues, swirling greens, and tasteful terracottas.[2] So, the e-waste stays out of landfills, graffiti artists get to be creative (without fear of arrest), and you get the perfect pot for your pansies. Now that's an idea that can grow on you.
www.terracycle.net

A Big Stink

Ever wonder just how much one country tosses in the trash every year? Well, plug your nose for this one. According to Statistics Canada, Canadians produced 27,249,178 tons of waste in 2006[3], and managing all that trash costs municipalities more than two billion dollars a year.[4] The United Kingdom generated more than 220-million tons of household, commercial, and industrial waste in 2004.[5] And in the United States, the Environmental Protection Agency (EPA) reports Americans produced more than 250-million tons of trash in 2006.[6] Whoa, now that stinks!

❝ For Tom Szaky, the boy wonder with the big dream, worm poop was turning to gold. ❞

holding a business plan contest, he and a buddy, Jon Beyer, decided to enter. Their idea, to put it simply, was to turn worm poop into a liquid, bottle it, and sell it as plant fertilizer.

No, the guys didn't win that contest. They placed fourth. But for them, the whole exercise opened up one huge can of worms. (Sorry. Couldn't resist.) Tom and Jon decided to set up a business in the cluttered basement of an old office building. "We started trying to figure out how to make lots of worm poop," says Tom, who quit Princeton and maxed out his credit cards getting TerraCycle off the ground. "That was the first step. We built a big system to do that. And then it was going and meeting with retailers and seeing if we could get anyone to pick it up."

Later, Tom entered and won a national business plan competition hosted by a venture capital company. The prize was — brace yourself for this — a million dollars in start-up money. Even though he had only 500 bucks in the bank at the time, Tom decided to say "No thanks" to the hunk of cash. He just didn't feel right about the

ideas the company had for TerraCycle's future. He wanted to be in charge.

Which was probably just as well. Because not long after that, TerraCycle got another big break. The Home Depot started selling TerraCycle plant food on its website. Before long, other huge retail chains were selling the liquid wonder. Even Wal-Mart, the world's largest corporation, started stocking it. For Tom Szaky, the boy wonder with the big dream, worm poop was turning to gold. TerraCycle was on its way. "We're in 15,000 stores across North America," Tom says. "The business, at this point, is valued at about $35-million."

Tom likes to call his story a "revolution in a bottle." (In fact, that's the title of his book about TerraCycle's success.) Actually, there are lots of different bottles these days. Besides its original worm poop plant food, TerraCycle now cranks out fertilizers formulated for orchids, herbs, roses, and other plants. The company has lots of other products too — there's everything from fire logs to bathroom cleaners to wild bird feeders. TerraCycle even makes Christmas ornaments and backpacks. Every bit of it is eco-friendly to the extreme. "We have a huge range of

TRASHY BUSINESS

Tom Szaky of Terracyle, Inc., isn't the only big-time garbage man in the United States. A New York-based company called RecycleBank is cashing in on trash – and helping its customers get free stuff in the process. All you do is load your recyclables into a special bin and leave it on your curb. Then, you get 2.5 RecycleBank points for every pound of paper, plastic, and other stuff in the bin. You can use the points to get discounts at stores like Sears and Target.[7] RecycleBank has offices in the United States, the United Kingdom, and Canada.[8] You can get the company's whole trashy story at www.recyclebank.com.

> **❝ TerraCycle has graduated from a dorm room idea to a major player in green business. Like the plants that eat up its fertilizers, the company just keeps growing and growing. ❞**

different products at this point, all made from garbage," Tom says. "And that became the unifying element for us: making products from garbage."

Tom's unique — and highly lucrative — brand of trash talk impressed 50 students who gathered to hear his lecture in an amphitheater at the Harvard Business School one day. "When I walked into the presentation room, 10 minutes before Tom's speech was to begin, I wasn't sure what to expect," says Peter Escher, a Harvard MBA student. "Tom strikes me as a blend of entrepreneurial zeal and genuine intellectual curiosity. I really enjoyed my time and I imagine our paths will cross again in the future. He inspired a lot of students at Harvard Business School with his message."

But Tom's biggest fan is his wife, Soyeon Lee, an elegant classical pianist and environmentalist. (You can read her story in Chapter 11 of this book.) When she performed at Carnegie Hall in a designer gown made of more than 6,000 used juice pouches, Tom was there to cheer her on. "I have never seen Tom self-conscious about anything," Soyeon says. "He believes 200 percent in what he does, and he doesn't let negativity get in the way. He doesn't let tradition or 'the way it's done' or other people's expectations get in the way of his vision and his passion. I think he approaches his business with so much faith and love that he ultimately attracts success."

Tom's company has offices in Atlanta, Toronto, and Trenton, New Jersey. There's a factory in California. And four farmers are

under contract to produce tons of worm poop. TerraCycle has graduated from a dorm room idea to a major player in green business. Like the plants that eat up its fertilizers, the company just keeps growing and growing. "I'm not wealthy personally yet," Tom says. "But it's very different from being in college. Running a business and running around, raising money. What I think is unique is that every year, I walk into a different company because the company has doubled in size ... We want to end up being a billion-dollar business."

A billion dollars based on garbage? Somehow, it's not hard to believe Tom Szaky can do it.

PUSHING THE RIGHT BUTTONS

Where do old cell phones go to die? Into the backs of people's junk drawers, mostly. According to a UK-based group called Global Cool, a staggering 90-million unused mobile phones are lying abandoned in drawers and cupboards. Global Cool and Vodafone are trying to do something to stop this mobile madness. They're collecting donated phones and chargers, refurbishing them, and redistributing them around the world. Phones that can't be reused are taken apart and recycled. So far, Global Cool has received more than 100,000 phones and chargers.[9] The whole thing has a nice ring to it, don't you think?

www.globalcool.org

Kid Stuff

MAIA GREEN, Director, FUN (Friends Uniting for Nature) Camps

Moms and dads come in all shapes, sizes, and levels of coolness. But what would you think if your folks pulled you out of school, bought a sailboat, and hit the waves of the South Pacific for almost a year of nonstop adventure?

Fantasy, right? Not for Maia Green. Cruising with her parents and two sisters was amazingly, unforgettably, oh-so fabulously real. "My parents are awesome," she says, laughing. "Yeah, they're really awesome. They basically decided it was more of a learning experience to be in these different countries."

It all started when Maia was eight years old. Her dad was offered a job at a university in Fiji in the South Pacific. After three years living in the island nation, the family decided to set sail, turning their boat into a heavenly home school on the high seas. "We'd collect all sorts of things and really study the country we were in," says Maia, who spent time in New Zealand, New Caledonia, and French Polynesia during her year on the ocean. "I learned so much from traveling."

Maia is now a 27-year-old entrepreneur in Vancouver. She founded FUN (Friends Uniting for Nature) Camps, which gives kids hands-on learning about the environment and sustainable ways of living. "Ninety percent of the time is spent outside," says Maia, who discovered her love of working with kids when

she had a job at an after-school program. "We have a hike day where we hike through the woods, and we do a whole bunch of nature connections, and we hike down to the beach. We play various games. And we have a scavenger hunt on the beach, which also doubles as a beach clean-up. We go swimming, and we play catch in the water."

Maia Green was one green kid — to the extreme. When she was traveling in the South Pacific, she and some friends started the Green Club. "We decided that if we started a club with all our friends, it would suddenly be an international club all the way around the entire world," says Maia, who wrote a letter about global warming to the president of the United States when she was 11 years old. "Therefore, we would be able to just save the world. It seemed very simple."

When the Green family moved back to Victoria, Maia quickly became known as the "environmental one" at school. And then, when she was about 15 years old, a bunch of rubber ducks and one polluted creek showed her just how much power a teenager can have.

Bowker Creek was once a beautiful place where people swam and salmon spawned. But by the 1990s, much of the creek was enclosed in pipes or choked with garbage. Frustrated, Maia and some friends went to city council and demanded action.

But she didn't stop there. Maia led the first annual Bowker Creek Clean-Up and Rubber Duck Race. She raised money by selling rubber ducks, and hundreds of people turned out to watch the

> **❝ ... money was tight. Maia couldn't even pay herself. But when she saw the impact the program was having on the kids, it was worth it. ❞**

little toys "race" up the creek. Volunteers waded into the water and hauled out old bikes and loads of other junk. And the community came to see Bowker Creek as an important part of the ecosystem. Maia's first big eco-leadership project was a success.

"It was really fun," she says. "That's when I started to realize how much I loved it and could actually accomplish real things. Part of what made it really successful was that people were impressed by my age, so it ended up being on the front page of the paper. And I'm sure that was what helped to bring out so many people."

That kind of green activism, as Maia learned, can have many rewards. Because of her community service and high grades, she won a Canada Millennium Excellence Award, which meant Can$4,000 per year for her four years of environmental studies. There were loads of other, smaller scholarships too — so many that she had enough extra cash to take a trip to Greece and Italy. (Sweet!)

Maia always wanted to start her own business. And on the first day of FUN Camps, she was ecstatic as children arrived at her rented room at the University of British Columbia. "It was pretty

amazing," she says. "I was pretty much grinning from ear to ear all day!"

During the first year of FUN Camps, money was tight. Maia couldn't even pay herself. But when she saw the impact the program was having on the kids, it was worth it. She says she feels warm and fuzzy remembering one keen, inquisitive 11-year-old boy. His mother, Christine, was disabled and raising her son by herself. At the end of the summer, she sent an e-mail to Maia.

"Thank you for all your support with my son," Christine wrote. "It means more than I can ever say. You have no idea how valuable you have been in his life. He came to you a quirky boy with ideas and questions. And for the first time in his life, someone besides his parents listened and helped him figure things out. You have given him wings, and for that I will always be grateful."

Maia plans to help many more kids take flight in the years ahead. With FUN Camps now in bloom, she's offering spring break camps and an after-school program. She has even started FUN Links, a program that connects high school students with non-profit environmental organizations. "It's really exciting," Maia says. "It's exactly what I've always dreamed of."

GREENING UP YOUR BUSINESS DEGREE

What? Study finance and field ecology at the same time?

If you enroll in the Environment & Business program at the University of Waterloo in Canada, you certainly can. The program, the only one of its kind in North America, prepares students for green-soaked careers in everything from small businesses to multinational corporations.

"We take people who have a strong understanding of environmental principles, concepts, and practices and train them to work in the corporate world," says Mark Seasons, the associate dean of undergraduate studies in the Faculty of Environment. "They learn about green marketing, green entrepreneurship and corporate responsibility."

So where are the program's graduates? They're working for big banks, car manufacturers, oil companies, and even the United Nations. "There's a whole range of employers who are picking them up," Professor Seasons says. "It's just good business. It's good business to do things in an environmentally appropriate way."

You can read more about Waterloo's Faculty of Environment, which has eight different undergraduate programs, at www.environment.uwaterloo.ca.

Spotlight Feature

The Biggest Thing Since Fire?

Dr. Jim White, Professor, University of Colorado at Boulder

Are we living in the most interesting time on Earth since the discovery of fire?

Dr. Jim White thinks so.

"It is a weighty statement, and I don't say it lightly," says Dr. White, who teaches geological sciences and environmental studies at the University of Colorado at Boulder (CU-Boulder). "In terms of our relationship with this planet, it's a watershed event. It's the defining generation."

Until now, Dr. White says, every generation looked at the environment as being infinite, while today's youth — and all future generations — have to see the environment as having limits.

> ❝ 'There's a great deal of money to be made in dealing with environmental problems ...' ❞

"I can't stress how important a point in human history that is," he says. "And (young people) know that. I think they get that. And consequently, the environment is going to be a big part of their lives from now on. Living sustainably will be an issue from now on."

Dr. White admits to feeling a bit of sadness over the whole thing. He says his peers knew about environmental problems 20 or 30 years ago, but most of them didn't act on it. Back then, green was just a color, not a way of life.

"I am not happy with my generation that we did not step up and take this on," he says. "I think we had the opportunity to be one of the greatest

generations, to take on one of the bigger problems, and we have instead stuck our heads firmly in the sand with our butts up in the air."

But while young people are inheriting plenty of ecological ills, there's also a bright side — and it's decorated with dollar signs.

"There's a great deal of money to be made in dealing with environmental problems," Dr. White says. "And I don't think we have scratched the surface of that. As we recognize better that we are on an unsustainable path — we have to get back to sustainability — I think that's going to open up the door economically for a ton of opportunity."

CU-Boulder's environmental studies program has about 600 undergraduate students, Dr. White says. The university also offers graduate students the opportunity to blend environmental studies with journalism, law, or business. CU graduates have gone on to careers in communications, education, renewable energy, and many other areas.

In the past, Dr. White says, young people often faced a moral dilemma when it came to their working lives. Would you pick the job that made you the most money? Or, would you choose something that would put a smile on your face? A green career can remove that conflict.

"You can make good money *and* you can do good things," Dr. White says. "And it's fun to be able to say you can do both."

You can read more about environmental studies at CU-Boulder at http://envs.colorado.edu/about/.

A Little Carbon Sense

ROBERT NIVEN, President, Carbon Sense Solutions, Inc.

You think you know cold? You don't know real cold. Unless you live in Antarctica with the penguins. At the North Pole with Dasher and Blitzen. Or in Tuktoyaktuk, with the people who call the Canadian Arctic home.

Tuktoyaktuk ain't Tampa Bay. You don't see tourists flying in by the planeload and lounging poolside with pink drinks. At night in the wintertime, Tuktoyaktuk can get as cold as minus-50 degrees Celsius. That's minus-58 Fahrenheit. (Whoa. Grab your earmuffs.)

Either way you look at it, just thinking about that kind of cold can give you the shivers.

That's why it's so cool that some people really do go to "Tuk" as tourists. With its dogsleds, northern lights, and mesmerizing midnight sun, the hamlet of 956 people attracts those bold, brave, busting-for-adventure types of tourists.

Like Rob Niven, for example. He had his share of heat fighting forest fires in northern British Columbia when he was a university student. But in his early 20s, he decided it was time to chill in Tuktoyaktuk. The courageous Canuck and a friend spent a few weeks snowshoeing, hiking, and driving around the amazing little town on the upper edge of the Earth.

And then, one night, Rob got into a very icy jam. "Our truck broke down because it was just too cold," he says. "We had nowhere to

❝ The 31-year-old is in the business of making the stuff that spews out of factory smokestacks cleaner and less harmful to the environment. ❞

turn. Then someone came by and asked to help. An Inuit family took us in, and we stayed with them for two weeks and had a great time. I was able to sit in on a jamboree, eat whale blubber, and learn how to hunt. It was something else."

But it wasn't all fun and feasts. The Inuit people told Rob about their worries over the environment. Offshore oil and gas exploration was expanding in the Arctic. There were toxins in the fish. The shoreline was eroding in summertime. Weather patterns were becoming harder to predict. And while the rest of the world was talking about climate change, the people of the far north were beginning to feel it.

Rob, a travel junkie who has been to around 30 countries, had equally powerful experiences in a place that's as hot as Tuk is cold. While he was visiting sub-Saharan Africa, families in Mali and Senegal took him into their homes and shared their lives with him. Village chiefs told him sad stories of droughts and crop failures. "All throughout the region," Rob says, "these types of stories emerged."

Rob's global gallivanting gave him a good dose of green inspiration. Today, he's an environmental engineer living in Halifax, the biggest city on Canada's east coast. And partly because of what he learned in the freezing Arctic and the blistering African desert, he's devoting his career to fighting climate change. "It's wonderful," Rob gushes. "I love my job. I really do. And it's so motivating. I don't have any problem waking up in the morning and going to work."

Rob is president of Carbon Sense Solutions, Inc. He started the company three years ago, not long after graduating with a master's degree in environmental engineering. The 31-year-old is in the business of making the stuff that spews out of factory smokestacks cleaner and less harmful to the environment. He specializes in one of the hottest, fastest-growing areas in engineering right now: Carbon capture and storage (CCS).

"It's essentially a technology that buys us time to continue using fossil fuels while we develop a renewable energy infrastructure," Rob explains. "It captures carbon dioxide at the point of combustion. So when you're burning fossil fuel like coal, or anything that's dirty, you capture the CO_2 there and you transport it to a suitable storage site. The storage can be a number of things. Most of the discussion now is putting it back underground where it came from. So that's what it is in a nutshell."

CLEAN ENERGY CLEANS UP

There's already big growth in clean energy jobs in the United States. According to a non-profit organization called the Pew Charitable Trusts, jobs in America's "clean energy economy" grew 9.1 percent between 1998 and 2007. During the same period, traditional jobs grew by only 3.7 percent.[10]

So why is this technology important? Well, carbon dioxide is considered a potent cause of global warming. And Rob's technology means less of the stuff goes into the atmosphere. So, Rob's "carbon sense" solution makes common sense to a lot of people, and his business is beginning to boom. He does consulting work for governments and big corporations all over

> **❝Rob is dreaming big. Very big. If he gets his way, his technology will revolutionize the massive, multi-billion-dollar concrete industry.❞**

the planet. He goes to almost every United Nations Climate Change Conference. And the prime minister of Norway has even invited him to come talk about how carbon capture and storage can be expanded in that country.

But when Rob isn't jet-setting, he's passionately developing his own concrete ideas. Literally. Rob has invented a system that takes carbon dioxide waste gases and adds them to concrete. The idea, of course, is that less pollution would puff out of smokestacks. But as a mega-sized bonus, carbon dioxide can actually be used to make better, stronger pre-cast concrete. "It's not as though the CO_2 is a gas that's traveling through the concrete," Rob explains. "It's actually stored as limestone, a mineral ... You're creating limestone because that's the chemical product when you react CO_2 with cement."

Rob is dreaming big. Very big. If he gets his way, his technology will revolutionize the massive, multi-billion-dollar concrete industry. Concrete manufacturers around the world are under pressure to curb their greenhouse gas emissions. At the same time, they're always looking for ways to make better concrete. Rob believes his system is the answer. "When you're convincing concrete users to bring this technology into the process, you don't even need to talk to them about greenhouse gas reduction because there are so many other benefits," he says. "It reduces the amount of energy they use,

it reduces the amount of time it takes to make concrete, and it makes their concrete stronger. It really has concrete — pardon the pun — benefit."

Rob's technology isn't on the market yet. But a company in rural Nova Scotia is putting it to the test, capturing carbon from its own factory and mixing it into concrete. Rob says carbon-fortified concrete cures faster, develops fewer cracks, and absorbs less water. "Once we work out the bugs, it's going to be a real fun ride," he says. "We're going to try to deploy this to as many people who are willing to take it on as possible. We see it as our contribution to reducing global greenhouse gases."

And for Rob, that's what it comes down to. Making a difference. Improving the world. And earning bucks at the same time. In the eco-loving 21st century, that's the kind of green career that gets a lot of folks excited. "People have wanted to come on and work with me or collaborate on things," Rob says, "just because they see it as a way they can actually have some sort of significance."

On the practical side of things, green technology is a great place to be if the economy bottoms out. Even when other industries come crashing down, carbon capture just keeps growing and growing. "This is one sector that is recession-resistant," Rob says. "There's a lot of money right now being devoted to it. This is one of the leading green techs."

And on top of all that, Rob loves the freedom of being his own boss. As an up-and-coming entrepreneur, he can work wherever — and whenever — he likes. "You don't need to work in an office in a high tower," he says. "You can work with a laptop in a coffee shop if you want, and there's many days I do that. There's no stigma there. You can do whatever you want."

In Rob's wildest dreams, his carbon-to-concrete technology will reduce hundreds of megatons of greenhouse gases around the planet each year. That won't stop climate change. But to him, it's one very big step. "There's a great deal of interest in this technology," he says. "It will have a really big impact on this world."

That kind of ambition must be cast in stone. Or concrete, at least.

URBAN
GREEN

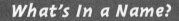

What's In a Name?

TREE STURMAN, Horticulturalist

You can't tell the story of Tree Sturman without first telling the story of his wonderful name.

❝ 'My lifelong mission,' Tree explains, 'is to try to reform education so that it serves the passion inside all people to connect to something bigger than themselves. And nature is that perfect thing. It's so broad, so big, so beautiful.' ❞

Twenty-nine years ago, a young couple had a baby boy. The mother wanted to name him Tristan. But the father wouldn't hear of it. So they decided to make up a name: Treenan.

When Treenan was growing up in New York State, kids picked on him because of his unique name. But then something remarkable happened. When other children were watching TV or playing basketball, Treenan was exploring the woods behind his house. A shy boy, he loved his privacy and space. The birds, trees, and plants felt like friends. Communing with nature came, well, naturally.

And so, before long, the boy who fell in love with nature became known as "Tree." When Tree grew into a teenager, his parents wanted him to go to Cornell University, but Ivy League schools didn't impress him. He decided to move to Maine, where he spent five years at the College of the Atlantic (COA), a tiny university that's big on nature. All students at COA major

36

in human ecology, the study of people's relationship with the environment. "COA is a really fascinating and wonderful place," he says. "I could talk about that forever."

Tree's passion for plants took him to many other amazing places, from the spectacular gardens of millionaires to a river restoration project with ex-convicts in the Bronx. Now, he is Science Education Manager at the Chicago Botanic Garden, a 385-acre fantasyland of water lilies, swans, butterflies, grapevines, and beautiful blooms. There are thousands of trees around him, from the redtwig dogwoods of the Japanese Garden, to the adorable little bonsais, to the great old oaks of the McDonald Woods.

And in this perfect place, Tree does important work with city kids and teens, helping them see, and enjoy, the magic of Mother Nature. "In my building, there are four classrooms," says Tree, who earned a master's degree in horticulture before starting his job at the Garden. "It's loud all the time. We have hundreds of kids there. We serve about 30,000 kids each year. They'll come on field trips, or we'll do outreach programs in the community."

SCREEN TALK

In the old days – and I mean the really old days, before TV was invented – it was just assumed that young people would spend most of their time outside. The indoors, a dull, detestable thing to be avoided at all costs (at least for some teens!), was for eating and sleeping. These days, Mother Nature has big competition from part-time jobs, cell phones, video games, the malls, and television. Statistics Canada reports boys aged 15–19 watched an average of 2.6 hours of TV each day in 2005. Girls in the same age group watched 2.2 hours a day.[1]

uP ON THE ROOF

Now here's one way to send business through the roof. Or onto the roof, anyway. Green Roof Safari is a European company that takes tourists on green roof study tours. (Green roofs, in case you haven't heard of them, are roofs at least partly covered with soil and plants. Some even have trees.) One of the partners in the company is Christine Thuring, a young Swiss-Canadian with a master's degree in horticulture.[2] For just under US$4,000[3], you get a six-day tour of some of Europe's greatest, greenest rooftops, including the Basel Convention Centre and a zero-impact housing development.[4] www.greenroofsafari.com

Tree's name is a better-than-perfect fit. He has dedicated his career to inspiring people to be closer to nature. "My lifelong mission," he explains, "is to try to reform education so that it serves the passion inside all people to connect to something bigger than themselves. And nature is that perfect thing. It's so broad, so big, so beautiful."

As Tree sees it, there is a huge need for more nature in kids' lives these days. Many children, he says, have little or no chance to run and play outside. In some parts of Chicago, where gun violence and teen murders are a grim reality, life is about survival. "These kids are living under circumstances where you watch your back," Tree says. "What they're worried about is avoiding the gangs and the wrong crowd. The last thing they're worried about is learning. And even further from that is the environment."

But there are great moments, like when Tree went to speak with students at a school in a rough, run-down part of Chicago. Security was so tight it took him fifteen minutes just to get into the building. Once he was inside, he met two teenaged girls who had been inspired by

an environmental studies course. "They had never been interested in the environment," Tree says. "I don't think they could identify a squirrel from a raccoon. But they took that course and found it intriguing, so they ended up creating an environmental club for that school."

Tree says his greatest success story is Miguel, a bright teenager who lost his direction in life and started having trouble at school. When Miguel failed a class in environmental science, his teacher sent him to Tree. "This kid liked writing," Tree says. "He was interested in nature, but he couldn't get focused. And to make matters worse, his father died, so everything was just falling apart around him. I kind of took to him because you could see that spark inside of him. He just had a really good soul."

Tree is in charge of the Fairchild Challenge, a big environmental contest for youth at the Chicago Botanic Garden. As part of that, he hosts an eco-poetry slam, where teens get up and rock the audience

❝ 'I can light that first spark. I try to light as many fires as I can and keep them burning as brightly as I can. You can really make a difference in people's lives.' **❞**

HIGH AND MIGHTY IN CHI-TOWN

Chicago is known as the birthplace of skyscrapers. But all that concrete and steel is getting greener – and leafier. Just take a peek at the top of the 11-story Chicago City Hall. This revolutionary rooftop dazzles with 20,000 plants of more than 100 species, including shrubs, vines, flowers, and even a couple of trees. Like all green roofs, it improves air quality, absorbs rainwater, and provides a habitat for birds and insects. And because it absorbs less heat than an ordinary roof, the green rooftop keeps City Hall cooler in the summer.[5]

with their greatest, greenest poems. Miguel decided to give the slam a try — and ended up winning second prize.

Stoked by that success, Miguel and some friends went on to compete at Chicago's huge teen poetry festival, Louder Than A Bomb. They placed in the middle of the pack — and that's not bad at all for a brand-new team. Soon after that, Tree asked Miguel to be master of ceremonies for an event at the Botanic Garden. "Miguel just loved it and did an amazing job," Tree says. "His environmental science teacher, who had failed him twice, was there cheering him on and was so moved at how he had changed and grown."

Miguel, now a high school graduate, describes Tree as a truly caring person and an unsung hero. "Tree has made one of the biggest differences in my life," Miguel says. "I now am pursuing a career as a writer, and I owe it in large part to Tree. He introduced me to slam poetry through the Fairchild Challenge. And frankly, I haven't looked back since. Through his work, he reached out to me, and my life was changed for the better."

Tree married his wife, Elaine Grehl, at a marsh surrounded by beautiful trees. (Of course!) She says one of the things that makes him unique is his refusal to be hindered by the status quo. "His strength to defend the environment is so admirable," Elaine says. "Tree truly and passionately believes that all lives on Earth are intentional blessings, that the life of a squirrel or an oak has no more or less value than a human life. Tree's demand for respect for nature is unwavering."

Years after discovering the beauty of nature as a boy in the woods, Tree is loving his career as an environmental educator. And as time goes on, he wants to keep connecting kids with the environment, helping them to believe in themselves, and inspiring them to dream. "Through the work that I do," he says, "I can light that first spark. I try to light as many fires as I can and keep them burning as brightly as I can. You can really make a difference in people's lives."

BRANCHING OUT IN NYC

Who says the concrete jungle can't have a few leaves? The mayor of New York City has a plan to plant one million trees by 2017. No, Mayor Bloomberg isn't doing all the digging himself! As part of the MillionTreesNYC program, the city is teaching a select group of young New Yorkers about tree care, ecological restoration, landscape design, and gardening. Ultimately, the city's urban forest is expected to expand by 20 percent. Many of the tree-loving trainees, meanwhile, will go on to have green-collar careers.[6] Now that's a blooming good idea, Mayor Bloomberg!

www.milliontreesnyc.org

Spotlight Feature

A Degree In Green

David Hales, President, College of the Atlantic

It seems fitting that the College of the Atlantic (COA) is on Eden Street. Sitting on 35 acres along the rocky coast of Mount Desert Island in Maine, the internationally renowned, Earth-loving school is its own kind of paradise.

"There's almost no place on campus that you can't see either the bay or the North Atlantic," says David Hales, president of COA. "I love coming to work."

❝ 'I think if there is a common trait in the students, it is a belief that they, as individuals, can make a difference," Hales says. "They want to make life better. These are particularly purposeful kids. They are ones that are looking for both the educational underpinning and a set of practical skills that will allow them to follow through on their dreams.' ❞

COA is a magnet for students who want their education drenched in green. The college has no departments or formal majors. Instead, it offers only one degree: a Bachelor of Arts in human ecology. With its broad, interdisciplinary approach, COA teaches students about everything from history and art to physics and chemistry.

"In its essence," Hales explains, "human ecology expresses a recognition that humans are part of the environment. We interact with it. It's within our discretion to choose the nature of that relationship. So it's important to understand what human actions do to the environment and vice versa."

COA offered its first class in 1972, with only four full-time instructors and 32 students. It was the first college in the United States to make the relationship between humans and nature its main focus. That mission has never changed, but the college now has 30 faculty members and more than 300 students.

"I think if there is a common trait in the students, it is a belief that they, as individuals, can make a difference," Hales says. "They want to make life better. These are particularly purposeful kids. They are ones that are looking for both the educational underpinning and a set of practical skills that will allow them to follow through on their dreams."

COA is a close-knit community where everybody is on a first-name basis. Some universities pack hundreds of students into monumental lecture halls, but most classes at COA have around 12 students. It's not unusual to see classes at COA being held along the shoreline, in the bogs, or by the trees. Many students take weekend hikes at nearby Acadia National Park.

At COA, human ecology is not just something to study. It's a way of life. COA is one of the first carbon-neutral colleges in the country. The college grows its own organic potatoes, carrots, and other foods on the Beech Hill Farm. All of the coffee on campus is organic and fair trade. The college's paper is completely chlorine-free. The wood used in construction on campus is from forests that are managed in a sustainable way. The residences have composting toilets. And all of COA's electricity is produced by renewable hydropower. No wonder Forbes.com calls COA "the greenest college in the land."[7]

❝ 'The simple truth is that any college that is not carbon-neutral is going to have a real tough time competing for new students.' ❞

"We really try to behave consistently with what we teach," Hales says. "The simple truth is that any college that is not carbon-neutral is going to have a real tough time competing for new students. And any college which is not heavily reliant on renewable energy is going to be wasting money that none of us can afford to waste."

So what do you do with a degree in human ecology? Just about anything, really. One COA graduate is vice president of a huge aquarium. Others run green restaurants in ultra-touristy Bar Harbor, Maine. Some have represented the

Environmental Protection Agency before the Supreme Court. Others start world-class businesses. (Ever hear of Newman's Own Organics, the company that makes pretzels, cookies, teas, and other all-natural treats? Former COA student Nell Newman, the daughter of movie legend Paul Newman, is the company's co-founder and president.)

Graduates of COA gush about the greatness of the little green university by the sea. "I had good grades in high school, so I could go just about anywhere I wanted to," says Nicole Cabana, a young pilot with the National Ocean and Atmospheric Administration (NOAA). (You can read the story of her high-flying adventures in Chapter 9.) "The more I looked at traditional schools, the more I didn't want that, and the more I wanted something different. I wanted to be in a place that was fully involved in making a difference and being environmental, and that's what I found at COA. Once I found COA, I didn't look anymore. I didn't apply anywhere else."

COA attracts plenty of international students, with about a fifth of the student body coming from outside the United States. "I think we have a curriculum and a college that does help prepare people who want to go back to their countries and improve things," Hales says, "whether it's on the social justice front, whether it's on environmental sustainability, or whether it's economic development and providing jobs."

Green careers, Hales says, demand a high level of excellence. "If any of us want to work with trying to move society to a sustainable relationship between humans and nature, that's a very complex task," he explains. "Just wanting to make it happen is not enough. You've got to learn the communication skills, you've got to learn your language skills, you've got to do your math, you've got to take the chemistry. And you've got to be better than anyone else. That's much more than just taking good intentions and trying to turn it into a career. It's hard work, and it's important to prepare for it."

Young people are finding plenty of ways to get ready to take on the world. But one option, at least, is to spend a few years on an idyllic island earning a degree in green.

Green-Collar Connections

JULIAN MOCINE-McQUEEN, Field Organizer, Green For All

A few years ago, Julian Mocine-McQueen was doing odd jobs in San Francisco, goofing off, and trying to figure out what to do with his life.

Oh, how things have changed. Julian now sees himself as part of a kind of revolution. It's a movement that's trying to pull people out of despair, improve lives, and create hope. Julian is helping change the world — at least his corner of it — and build something great.

So how's he doing it?

Julian is a field organizer with Green For All, a national organization that believes a "clean energy economy" can improve the lives of all Americans. The group lobbies governments to put more money into green jobs, provides career training, helps people set up businesses, and educates the public about the power of the green economy. By working to create "green-collar jobs" across the country, Green For All says it's fighting poverty and pollution at the same time.

For 28-year-old Julian, going to work at the Green For All office in Oakland, California, isn't just about earning a living. It's about sharing a vision. "It's the coolest thing in the world," he says. "It's just unbelievable. I think what's so exciting is that people really, for the first time in a long time, see it as a paradigm-shifting opportunity and solution."

❝ Julian's passion for social justice and a green economy has its roots in his childhood. As a little boy in west Oakland, he lived just up the block from one of the most violent public housing projects in the city. ❞

Julian was a college student when he first heard about Green For All. He applied for a job with the organization just as a historic conference called *The Dream Reborn* was being set up in Memphis. Held on the 40th anniversary of the assassination of Dr. Martin Luther King, Jr., the event looked at solutions to global warming and poverty. "I was brought on to help bring that [conference] together," Julian says. "I had the absolute honor of reaching out to people around the country to ensure that they were able to come to that event."

Julian's passion for social justice and a green economy has its roots in his childhood. As a little boy in west Oakland, he lived just up the block from one of the most violent public housing projects in the city. His parents decided to move the family to Humboldt County on California's north coast. "I think it broke their heart to move away because they really loved Oakland," Julian says. "But they just felt like they had a choice to make."

So, Julian and his brothers grew up in the country, far from the drugs and murders of the city. Sometimes, his two cousins from Oakland would visit. "We'd just run around in the woods," Julian says. "We were right by a river, so we would go swimming and riding around on dirt bikes and stuff like that. I had a real clear sense of the value of being closer to nature, having the opportunity to sleep outside and know what a starry

night actually looks like without the pollution of all the lights in the city."

But the river couldn't wash all of the violence out of Julian's world. His two cousins got into trouble with the law and went to prison. And about 10 years ago, his uncle was shot and killed. "A random act of violence here in Oakland," Julian says. "That obviously hit close to home. He was robbed at a Kentucky Fried Chicken. Murdered. There was no sense behind it. Never solved. No clear motive other than the $30 that was there or something like that."

When Julian finished high school and moved to San Francisco, the murders and other violence in parts of the city continued to trouble him. In this world-class metropolis full of tourists, cable cars, and gleaming skyscrapers, he couldn't forget the people who were living in poverty and fear. "There's a small African-American minority, and there's a small Hispanic minority," he says. "These deaths are happening overwhelmingly in those communities across the board. They are being ignored, and that was really painful."

In his job with Green For All, Julian tries to help at least some Americans escape that pain. He connects people who want green jobs with organizations that can help them. He counsels budding green entrepreneurs. Sometimes, he even helps run the Green For All Academy, which trains

> ❝ In this world-class metropolis full of tourists, cable cars, and gleaming skyscrapers, Julian couldn't forget the people who were living in poverty and fear. ❞

47

community leaders and shows them how to spread the word about the green economy. "I just can't tell you how exciting it is," Julian says. "We are in a position to be able to link people together ... to help serve their work."

There are great green success stories across the United States. The City of Chicago, for example, runs Greencorps Chicago. It's a program that gives people, many of them ex-cons, training and jobs in horticulture. In the South Bronx, Green Worker Cooperatives helps set up environmentally friendly businesses. And in California, Solar Richmond teaches low-income residents how to install solar panels and helps them find jobs.

Julian says he feels privileged to be in such close contact with Americans who are doing good work. For the next year or two, he'll focus on being there for them, giving them the help they need to fulfill their green dreams.

"This is not a solution for one city to try to help curb some violence," he says. "This is a way to transform our entire society so that we are a less violent society and we are all better able to prosper. At the same time, we recognize and recapture the value in Mother Earth and take care of the land that we're on. I think that a lot of people see that vision."

Spotlight Feature

Hip-Hop Hope
Markese Bryant, Musician & Green Entrepreneur

Markese Bryant has come a long way since the day he was arrested for selling crack cocaine.

After his troubles with the law, the 24-year-old from Oakland, California, decided to go to college and major in African-American studies. Then, just seven months ago, he came across a YouTube clip that changed his whole outlook. It was a speech by the founder of Green For All.

"I didn't know who he was at the time," Markese says. "He started talking about green jobs and how we can lift people out of poverty and combat global warming at the same time. The part that really struck me was lifting people out of poverty. At that time, I didn't have a very good understanding of global warming."

Markese started doing research about green jobs and climate change. When he visited the Green For All office in Oakland, he was invited to attend two career conferences. He was so moved by the experiences he wrote "The Dream Reborn," a hip-hop tune about the green jobs movement. The people at Green For All liked the song — a lot. They're even making a music video for it, and they offered Markese (a.k.a. Doo-Dat) an internship. "I want to turn it into a hit," Markese says. "I really think the song has the potential to do that. That's really the main focus."

Markese will graduate from college next year, and he has big dreams of becoming a hip-hop star.

But this eco-emcee is a budding green entrepreneur too. If he makes it in music, he wants to invest in renewable energy. He's also starting a non-profit organization to help predominantly black colleges do green retrofits. In just a few months, Markese's life has changed.

"I'm the green dude, all of a sudden," he says with a laugh.

THE RED, WHITE, AND BLuE - AND GREEN!

Even the most powerful person in the world is on the green jobs bandwagon. During the U.S. presidential election campaign in 2008, Barack Obama vowed to spend $150-billion on clean energy over 10 years. That, he said, would end the nation's dependence on oil and create up to five million jobs.[8]

Planning and Pedaling

MATT LEE, Urban Planning Student

Matt Lee found his life's passion with a little inspiration from an overgrown electric Santa Claus.

It happened back in the 1980s, when Matt was a young boy living in the great, glittery metropolis of Hong Kong. The city, more than any other place on Earth, is a spectacle of thousands of shiny skyscrapers. And at Christmas, millions of colored lights strung on the giant buildings make megawatts of magic.

"I remember a Santa Claus, very brightly lit," says Matt, now a 25-year-old university student. "It was very elaborate, multi-colored, flashy."

When Matt was five, he and his family left Hong Kong to make a new life near Toronto, Canada. But he never forgot the neon Santa, the skyline, and the thrill of exploring a city of six million people.

Canada, of course, had its urban thrills too. Not long after arriving in the country, Matt made his first trip to the top of the amazing, 1,815-foot-tall (553 meters) CN Tower, one of the tallest man-made structures on Earth. "It was frightening, actually," he says. "I remember my ears getting plugged when I was going up on the elevator. Once I was up there, it was pretty phenomenal. You're no longer scared."

By the time Matt was in elementary school, he was using cardboard, construction paper, and paint to make little models of cities. "Sure, it wasn't really to scale or anything," he remembers. "It was definitely not a very impressive product, looking back at it. But that was kind of the first sign that this was something I wanted to do."

❝ Urban planning in the 21st century isn't just about concrete, steel, and the quest for monster profits. At the University of Waterloo, lots of emphasis is placed on making the planning profession as green as it can be. ❞

Matt has learned a lot since his childhood adventures with crude cardboard models. These days, he's an award-winning graduate student building his dream career in urban planning, a profession that focuses on developing communities in an orderly way.

He started with a Bachelor of Environmental Studies at the University of Waterloo, where students in the School of Planning learn about everything from economics and ecology to statistics and sociology. Soon, he will graduate with a Master of Arts in Planning. "My specialty in my master's is transportation planning," Matt says. "What's really great is that I'm with other

RADICAL RICKSHAWS

The rickshaw has turned into one funky ride! A German company called Velotaxi invented a sleek, curvy, futuristic-looking rickshaw with pedals. With its lightweight steel frame, half-reclining seat, and 21 gears, the company's CityCruiser is one bad-ass three-wheeler.[9] The cool contraptions are tearing up the streets in eco-friendly style in more than 45 communities around the globe.[10] Word has it the green warriors behind the wheel – er, handlebars – haul in good tips and have great legs too!

www.velotaxi.de

similar-minded people. We're part of a transportation research group."

Urban planning in the 21st century isn't just about concrete, steel, and the quest for monster profits. At the University of Waterloo, lots of emphasis is placed on making the planning profession as green as it can be. That means learning how to have a "built environment," like a city, while causing as little damage as possible to the natural environment.

"We're trying to reverse some of the things we've done in the past," Matt says. "I see consideration for the environment as increasingly relevant now, especially dealing with issues of climate change and personal health. We're definitely less active than we once were."

Matt and two of his classmates won national attention — and a nice chunk of cash — for one of their eco-friendly urban ideas. Inspired by bicycle-sharing programs in Barcelona and Paris, they came up with a proposal for a similar program for their city. The big difference with this new program is that it would be self-serve and high-tech. You could swipe a card and pick up a bike at a station, pedal to your destination, then leave it

at another station. That could mean fewer cars spewing pollution on the roads — and more people getting exercise. "It's a much speedier way to get around than walking," Matt says, "and it's environmentally sustainable."

Matt and his classmates summed up their bike-sharing ideas in a 2,000-word essay and entered it in the Go Green Challenge, a national contest sponsored by one of Canada's largest banks. Before long, they found out they had won the prize. "We were very, very shocked," Matt says. "In total, the prize was worth $25,000. Half of it would go to the university, and the other half would be shared among the three of us. We were astonished."

Professors and other staff at the university were thrilled about the team's big win. Jeff Casello, who teaches planning and civil engineering, describes Matt as a bright, energetic student. "I think what sets Matt apart from other students, other than his intelligence, is his awareness," says Casello. "When Matt walks around a city, he is always examining what works and what doesn't. Some of our best lessons are right in front of us — if we are open and curious enough to look for them."

After graduation, Matt hopes to go to work for a big public transit agency in Ontario. "If that doesn't pan out, I'm hoping to focus my career objectives in the transportation-planning field," he says. "That may be transportation consulting, or working for the public sector with transportation policy-related things."

Spotlight Feature

Teaching Green
Waddie Long, Faculty, Nova Scotia Community College

Things sure have changed since the 70s — and I'm not just talking about disco and shiny polyester man blouses.

Just ask Waddie Long. He started his environmental career when he was a young man in 1977. He left his native Nova Scotia to spend some time working in the forestry industry of British Columbia. But he couldn't believe — or accept — how so many huge trees were being cut down and left to rot on the forest floor.

One day, a co-worker on the logging operation snapped at Waddie, telling him to forget "that toothpick." The man was talking about a tree. Far from tiny, it was two feet (around half a meter) in diameter. "That really shook me up, seeing that," says Waddie, who now teaches at the Nova Scotia Community College (NSCC). "So I didn't stay there much longer after that."

Waddie went back to Nova Scotia and bought a 100-acre woodland. He started managing it his own way, not the industrial forestry way. To this day, the land attracts plenty of wildlife. There are even eagles, hawks, and owls nesting in the trees. "So I can't imagine doing anything else, you know what I mean?" Waddie says.

In 2005, Waddie helped launch a Natural Resources Environmental Technology program at the NSCC. There are courses on, among other things, climate change, environmental law, and entrepreneurship. "It's been hugely successful," he says. "We have a wait list every year. ... We didn't want to pigeonhole graduates into one job, so we made it so that they can follow their dream."

And graduates of the two-year program *are* finding their dream jobs. Waddie says one grad is a supervisor with a major international environmental company. Another young man is an aerial photo interpreter in British Columbia.

54

Waddie says it's great to know his former students are out there changing the world. "I see a student walk across that stage at graduation with their head up high," he says. "And then I see them a year, or two, or three years later. They come back and they have their dream job ... and they send me e-mails thanking me for helping them get their dream job. I'm getting goose bumps telling you."

Waddie says he sees great hope in today's young people. "I see a generation that cares," he says. "I don't see these young people as environmental activists. I see them as environmental *actionists*. They're not talking about it. They're doing it. ... An 18-year-old with 'environmental footprint' in their vocabulary is a big change."

The Smell of Success

ERICA STOLP, Environmental Technician

It can be a stinky job, but Erica Stolp is happy to do it.

The 23-year-old is an environmental technician with Rowan Williams Davies & Irwin Inc. (RWDI) in Guelph, Ontario. As an air quality expert, Erica spends much of her time at landfills and wastewater treatment plants. Sometimes, she even collects sacks of smelly air at a huge compost facility near Toronto.

"We actually fill 10 large bags with air that contain the odor," Erica says. "If the smell is unacceptable, the company has to do something to control their odor."

> 'You don't want to go to school for something and then not be able to get a job. So knowing that there are lots of jobs was a big deal. And everyone in my program who graduated has a job in our field.'

55

For Erica, finding a job was a big green cinch. After high school, she went to Fanshawe College in London, Ontario, to study environmental technology for three and a half years. It's a hands-on program that focuses on monitoring techniques for water and air. When Erica graduated, she didn't have a whiff of worry about her future. With "tons of opportunity" in the environmental field, she was offered a full-time job at RWDI even before she had her diploma.

❝ Erica Stolp, meanwhile, is loving the work at RWDI. In the summertime, she can be out in the field up to 90 percent of the time. ❞

"It was very nice," Erica says. "You don't want to go to school for something and then not be able to get a job. So knowing that there are lots of jobs was a big deal. And everyone in my program who graduated has a job in our field."

For someone just out of college, getting a job with RWDI Inc. is a bit of a coup. The company is one of the largest, most successful engineering firms in Canada. RWDI is well-known in engineering circles for its wind testing of famous structures like the Petronas Towers in Malaysia, the half-scale Eiffel Tower in Las Vegas, and the breathtakingly tall Burj Dubai skyscraper. The company has even been featured in glitzy TV documentaries.

But even for an engineering superstar like RWDI, finding enough workers is a feat. "We would like to grow at about 10 to 15 percent per year," says Mark Vanderheyden, a vice president at RWDI. "Finding the work is not the problem. It's finding the people."

As RWDI hunts for workers specializing in noise and vibration, air quality, pollution control, meteorology, and ventilation design, Fanshawe College is happy to crank out the next generation of environmental experts. "Our graduate employment rate is very high," says Cathy Gall, the coordinator of Environmental Technology and Science Laboratory Technology at Fanshawe. "Our students have great success finding employment in their applied field of study. Since our graduates have a minimum of 12 months and maximum of 16 months of co-op work experience when they complete the program, they are well-equipped for employment."

Erica Stolp, meanwhile, is loving the work at RWDI. In the summertime, she can be out in the field up to 90 percent of the time. Some of her co-workers are also young people who graduated from the same program. "It's nice to be working," she says, "and able to apply everything I learned."

Ah, the sweet smell (or stink, as the case may be) of success!

Chapter 3

BUILDING GREEN

From Misery to Bliss

STET SANBORN, Architect

Picture this. You're in your early 20s, you've just finished a degree in mechanical engineering, and one of the biggest automotive companies in the world can't wait to give you a job. You're a techie type who has always loved cars, especially that old red Volkswagen Fastback you tinkered with in high school, so you jump at the chance. Before long, you're designing calipers and rotors for shiny new SUVs and hot sports cars. And oh yes, the job pays a bundle. So what do you do?

Well, if you're Stet Sanborn, you quit.

Now don't get me wrong. Stet is no slacker. Quite the opposite, really. It's just that besides having a passion for all things technical, Stet has a strong, sincere, not-to-be-denied environmental conscience. Sure, he was making big bucks in the auto industry. But it just didn't feel right.

"You go into a plant, and you just see the vast quantity of steel being poured, and being machined, and all the energy that goes into it," says Stet, who's now 28. "And it was just sort of mind-boggling. At that point, I had no idea of the energy that got sucked into these manufacturing processes for a vehicle, which ultimately you typically drive by yourself short distances. And I think my discomfort with that just kept growing."

> ❝ ... he was making big bucks in the auto industry. But it just didn't feel right. ❞

> ❝ Stet's love for cars wore away like the treads of a tire. He didn't think he could stand to stay in the auto industry. ❞

59

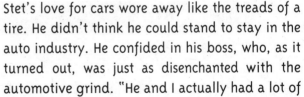

❝ ... Stet actually gets paid a little extra for biking eight miles to work. ❞

BIG IDEAS, TINY HOUSES!

Want to do something really big for the planet? How about taking up residence in a teensy-tiny house? Jay Shafer of the Tumbleweed Tiny House Company in Sebastopol, California, makes houses smaller than some people's closets! The funky mini-abodes feature peaked roofs, verandas, and fabulous colors. And what's more, you can green up your piddly pad with solar panels, compost toilets, and other eco-friendly additions.[1] (www.tumbleweedhouses.com).

A Canadian company called aerieLOFT, meanwhile, makes a 10-by-11-foot (3-by-3.35 meter), sail-shaped cedar home with high ceilings and a funky loft. You can stick the chic little chateau in your backyard or perch it by your fave fishing hole. No wonder the company calls the Aerie "one fancy-ass tent"![2] (www.aerieloft.ca)

Stet's love for cars wore away like the treads of a tire. He didn't think he could stand to stay in the auto industry. He confided in his boss, who, as it turned out, was just as disenchanted with the automotive grind. "He and I actually had a lot of frank conversations," Stet says. "We were both seeing that what we were doing wasn't making us happy inside. It was great for our paychecks, but not for our souls."

As Stet searched for a new kind of soul food, friends suggested he work on electric vehicles or fuel cells. He wasn't interested. It was time for a bigger change. So, Stet the engineer decided to become Stet the eco-architect. "All my friends who I had gone to school with were shocked," he says, laughing at the memory. "They weren't shocked that I wanted to go into architecture because that had been brewing for a while. But engineers are, especially in the auto industry, paid a lot better than architects."

Stet left Michigan, the mecca of motors, and headed west. He spent three years studying architecture at

the University of California at Berkeley, quickly learning that life really could be greener on the architectural side. He liked the fact that the program put a lot of emphasis on environmentally conscious design. To Stet, sustainable buildings made serious sense. "Ultimately, people will buy sustainability if they understand it," he says. "It's not just about energy. It's not just about materials. It's also about improving the quality of the experience, making a healthier building for healthier occupants. That's one of the big focuses at the school.

When Stet received his master's degree in architecture, he barely had time to admire the diploma before he started the job of his dreams. He joined Siegel & Strain Architects, an award-winning San Francisco firm that began championing green architecture way before it was considered cool. The company's long list of accomplishments includes straw

> ❝ 'What I'm working on are things that are really transformative, things that will last a hundred years.' ❞

bale buildings, an environmental camp for kids, and an energy-efficient science center overlooking a California river. Siegel & Strain is celebrated for its smart, stylish use of things like cork floor tiles, bathroom partitions made out of recycled yogurt containers, and solar panels. "It's really great to be here," says Stet, "because there's so much that I can learn from the work that they've been doing for 20 years."

For Stet, Siegel & Strain is a perfect fit. He works in a beautiful old brick building — he calls it a "living laboratory" — and his desk is made of recycled, ground-up husks. The firm is a big

booster of bicycling, and if you can believe it, Stet actually gets paid a little extra for biking eight miles to work. (How cool is that?)

Best of all, Stet loves his work. Right now, he's helping design a building that will be a "green escape" for the people of San Francisco. The structure, a stunning showcase of eco-friendliness, will have a plant nursery, classrooms, and offices. It will even maintain its own water supply, treating rainwater and toilet water with plant-based systems. "The real focus (of this building) is for youth," Stet explains. "It's for urban kids who maybe haven't gotten a chance to go out into the woods and see nature. It's right there in the city, but it feels like a world away."

Stet also worked on the design of a new community hall near the lush vineyards of California's wine country. The structure was built with lots of recycled materials. It has an ultra-modern natural ventilation system designed to reduce the need for noisy, electricity-devouring air conditioners. Even the concrete was mixed with waste materials from the power industry. In the end, the community hall will give people a better understanding of the benefits of sustainable design.

❝ 'You don't have to do exactly what you studied in school. Your education is the foundation for what you really want to do. Look for the things that really make you happy, and find programs that support that.' ❞

"I can't even compare how much happier I am now than I was as an automotive engineer," says Stet, whose devotion to the environment is so strong he takes Amtrak instead of flying across the country to visit

his relatives. "Just in terms of doing something that I can actually believe in. And I don't have guilt. It's like a guilt-free employment. What I'm working on are things that are really transformative, things that will last a hundred years.

Despite the happiness he's finding in green architecture, Stet says studying engineering was not a mistake. "The skills that I got studying engineering I still use every day," he explains. "It's just a different focus. I still look at energy systems. I still look at efficiency. There are still calculations. There's still heat transfer. All the things that I studied in engineering are completely applicable to building. And so I just sort of changed the line of sight from cars to buildings."

With more and more countries around the world now pushing eco-friendly design, Stet believes green architecture will keep on booming. "I think demand is just going to skyrocket as we see how important buildings are and how much energy they use," he says. "I think sustainability as a whole is just going to drive so many jobs, even outside the field of architecture."

Having made the journey from automotive misery to architectural bliss, Stet has advice for teens who are mulling over their career options. "Have your eyes open and follow what you really want to

BIG, GREEN, AND SHINY

According to Guinness World Records, the world's largest solar energy roof tops the Floriade Exhibition Hall in Haarlemmermeer, Netherlands. So just how big is this revolutionary roof? It's made up of more than 19,000 solar panels, and its total area is 281,045 square feet (26,110 square meters). To put that in perspective, the monstrous marvel is the size of more than four American football fields. Now that's one super solar spectacle![3]

do," he says. "I don't really regret going through engineering. It has helped me a lot. But the part that's most important is being aware that I didn't have to just do that. You don't have to do exactly what you studied in school. Your education is the foundation for what you really want to do. Look for the things that really make you happy, and find programs that support that."

And who knows? If you study architecture at Berkeley, Stet Stanborn just could be one of your profs. The university has invited him back to teach a course about energy systems for buildings.

To Stet, the purring engine of a sexy new sports car just can't compare with that kind of success.

The Nature of Architecture

REBECCA BRUCE, Sustainable Architect

As everyone knows, the little piggy who built a house of straw ended up with a raw deal.

> ❝ 'Architecture is a wonderful career if you're interested in incorporating lots of diverse subjects.' ❞

But if a similar piggy were to build a straw house today, the place might actually stand a chance of surviving the wrath of a blowhard wolf. It would score mega points on the eco-scale. And heck, Piggy could even get an architect to turn his little house into one chic chateau.

Yes, straw-bale construction is becoming fashionable in some nature-loving circles these days. Straw is environmentally friendly to the extreme. Termites don't have a taste for it, apparently. If it's done right, it can last thousands of years. And when it's covered in plaster or stucco, straw can look pretty cool.

So when Rebecca Bruce finished five intense years of studying architecture at the University of Kansas, she decided to put a hold on plunging into the world of concrete and steel. Instead, she spent more than a year doing a straw-bale internship with a non-profit organization called The Canelo Project in sweltering southern Arizona.

"I got muddy and got my hands dirty and did a lot of practical stuff," she says. "And I met a lot of people who are out there in the world wanting to build their own small house out of straw bale, a material they feel comfortable with. And that was really fun."

BIG, GREEN, AND WINDY

The wind energy industry is spawning a bunch of bodacious blades. The Enercon E-126 in Emden, Germany, is one of the biggest wind turbines on the planet. This rotating, power-making monster is 442.9 feet (135 meters) tall. That's more than one-third the height of the Eiffel Tower! And besides being an awesome sight to behold, this mega-machine packs a punch. E-126 generates enough clean energy to supply 5,000 four-person homes. That's one wild windmill![4]

The Canelo Project uses things like apple juice jars, olive oil soap, and linseed oil as building materials. With the help of her brother, her sister, and some friends, Rebecca built a straw-bale cabin in west Texas. "That was really the key in understanding how difficult construction is," she says. "It's

hard work and very complicated, very skilled. I think it takes really smart people to build buildings."

ECO-MOTIVATORS

So what's motivating people to go into environmental careers? The Environmental Careers Organization (ECO Canada) wanted to know. It surveyed more than 5,000 Canadians working in the environmental sector. "The number-one reason, when we surveyed young people, as to why they want to go into the environment is they want to make a difference," says Grant Trump, President and CEO of ECO Canada. "They believe that this is the right thing to do." The second-biggest attraction of green careers is the variety of jobs and duties, Trump says. And the third biggest attraction of working green? The opportunity to work outdoors.[5]

Straw must have looked good on Rebecca's resume. She was hired by LakelFlato Architects in San Antonio, Texas. It was a feat, really, for a new architect in her mid-20s. The American Institute of Architects, after all, named LakelFlato its Firm of the Year a few years ago. The firm is famous for modern, elegant designs that work with the environment. "We try to use a lot of simple materials," says Rebecca, who's now 27 years old. "And we try to do it in a very beautiful way."

Rebecca grew up in Kansas City, Missouri. She was a child who loved science classes, field trips, animals, and plants. In high school, she contemplated what kind of career would build on her passions. "I decided on architecture, which is a field where art and science can mix,"she says. "For me, that's really exciting because I enjoy the world of art. ... Architecture is a wonderful career if you're interested in incorporating lots of diverse subjects."

From the beginning of her studies, Rebecca knew she wanted to marry architecture to Mother Earth. She took a class on sustainability during her second year in university — and loved it. Eager and enthusiastic, she spent time with the professor, did research, and learned everything she could. "Sustainability is important," Rebecca says. "I'm a human being and I live on the planet, and I want to be the best human being I can be. I want to participate in a way that allows everything else in the world to participate. I care a lot about fresh water and trees and plants and animals. Not just for my use or consumption, but for all the other animals and plants that deserve to live just as much as I do."

Sustainable architecture takes an eco-friendly approach to cooling and heating. Some buildings, for example, have windows designed to draw in refreshing cross-breezes. That cuts down the need for noisy, electricity-hungry air conditioning. And in cold climates, buildings can be designed to take advantage of the warmth of the sun. "We try to look at how we can make a passive building," Rebecca says. "That's a building that works with the sun angles and the weather."

Building materials are just as important. LakelFlato avoids things like formaldehyde and PVC. Many of the firm's buildings are shining shrines to the glory of wood. "Some materials cost more carbon," Rebecca explains. "They are more energy-intensive to make, such as concrete. But then there are materials that use less embodied energy, like wood. And so there's a spectrum of really high carbon footprints and really low carbon footprints."

THE WORLD'S GREENEST?

So what's the world's greenest building? Independence Station in the town of Independence, Oregon, is the newest building to claim the title. The complex, with its condos, stores, offices, and classrooms, is a chic spectacle of renewable energy. The roof of Independence Station has solar panels, which will produce more than enough energy to run the building during sunny months. At cloudier times of the year, the building will be powered partly by used vegetable oil from local restaurants. Each condo at Independence Station has a state-of-the-art automatic indoor home composter, and residents will wash their clothes and flush their toilets with stored rainwater. The inside of the building even has a 40-foot (12.19-meter) vertical urban garden.[6] Home green home!

www.worldsgreenestbuilding.com

Rebecca is designing updates for a ranch in the mountains near San Diego. She's looking at adding wind turbines and rainwater collection. Stone for the construction will be quarried right at the site, not shipped in from China. Rebecca also helped design buildings, boardwalks, and trellises for the Naples Botanical Garden, a paradise of tropical gardens and restored natural habitats in Florida. The structures are made of a durable South American hardwood called ipe (pronounced E-pay). "We used it structurally and as a finish material," Rebecca says. "We tried to be really conscientious about the material we were using. Ipe lasts forever, kind of like a redwood, but it's not endangered."

Many of LakelFlato's star projects are green and gorgeous all over. Like a 400-acre arboretum in Maryland, a light-filled limestone synagogue in Texas, a stunning wood-and-stucco elementary school hugging a hill in California, and big, breezy ranch houses all over the southern United States. "The great

thing about working here is that the clients are on board with us," Rebecca says. "They come to us because they want what we do. We have to sell them a little bit, we have to educate them, we have to tell them some things. But by and large, they're really receptive, and they're here to work with us. It's a really healthy relationship."

Since she started working with LakelFlato, Rebecca has been making an impression on those clients — and her co-workers. "Rebecca has an enthusiasm and insatiable drive for everything she does," says Greg Papay, a partner in the firm. "As a design firm that pushes the integration of design with sustainability, our currency is ideas. And having someone like Rebecca, who is always interested in pushing that, is valuable and energizing....We see her as an important leader now and in the future for our firm."

DREAMS IN MOTION

If you like skyscrapers, this baby will blow you away. An architect named David Fisher has designed the world's first skyscraper in motion. Dynamic Tower is expected to be built in Dubai, the sparkling city of the United Arab Emirates. Unbelievably, each of the 80 stories of Dynamic Tower will be able to rotate independently. That means the shape of the skyscraper will constantly change! The spinning spectacle is just as green as it is bizarre. Photovoltaic cells, along with horizontal wind turbines mounted between the floors, will power the tower.[7] And what does it cost to live in this sky-high oasis? Luxury villas in Dynamic Tower could cost as much as $30-million. Now that's a lot of green.

www.dynamicarchitecture.net

Rebecca is all about creativity. And she loves the fact that her job lets her use that talent every day. "I enjoy coming into work and solving problems," she says. "It's kind of like every day

someone comes in and throws all these pieces down, and you figure out how to put them together. You do that for long enough, and you end up with these structures that are very complex. It's really a sense of accomplishment."

But for Rebecca, one of the best parts of the job is the knowledge that the buildings she's helping design aren't hurting the Earth. "I'm not interested in merely pursuing a way to make enough money to get by," she says. "I really want to do something that I feel strongly about, that I am engaged in. I want to be doing something that I care about."

With wood, stone, and the occasional bale of straw, Rebecca Bruce is building herself a bright green future in architecture.

A Budding Career

Carbon Neutral
JOSH KJENNER, *Mechanical Engineer*

AGE: 27

TITLE: Mechanical engineer with Manasc Isaac, an architecture firm specializing in carbon-neutral or "net-zero" buildings. "A net-zero building," Josh explains, "is basically a building that, over the course of a year, will generate as much energy as it consumes."

GREENSPIRATIONS: He grew up by a lake and spent time on the water with his brother and grandpa as a kid. He developed a strong environmental conscience in university, where his only humanities elective was a course about the philosophy of the environment.

THE FIRM: Manasc Isaac was one of the first architecture firms in Canada to adopt The 2030 Challenge, a global effort that commits architects and builders to greenhouse gas reduction.

GREEN IN MOTION: Manasc Isaac has a Green Transportation Plan. Employees who drive their own vehicles to work are charged a dollar per hour for parking. With the proceeds, the company buys bus passes for workers who choose to take public transit. Employees who walk or cycle to work get a $30 "walking subsidy" each month. An office fuel-efficient car is used for site visits and errands.

GREEN PROJECT: Josh worked on the Water Centre, a Can$43-million (US$40-million) eco-friendly building in Calgary. Partly because of the building's long, thin shape, 95 percent of its light comes from the sun.

THE REWARDS: "I just like the idea of contributing to a body of knowledge that can help to ensure the prosperity of future generations. It's really exciting for me to be a part of a new kind of movement where people are trying to figure out solutions to these really important problems."

ECO-ADVICE: "The thing that I found most useful is just kind of getting involved. Meeting people is the biggest thing. Meeting people who have worked in the field or who know people in the field. I think that there's really no substitute for talking to somebody who's been down the road before."

Chapter 4

THE
GREEN TICKET

Flight of the Green Angel

MELANIE MULLEN, Activist & Political Candidate

Many little girls love dressing up and pretending to be angels or fairies flitting about in the forest. And in their costume trunks or their pretty, sparkly dreams, the wings are usually purple or pink.

When Melanie Mullen was a child on the Canadian side of Niagara Falls, she had angel visions of her own. But as she closed her eyes and imagined herself in flight, her wings were a different color.

"The wings were dyed green so that I could spread that green across the Earth," she says. "I wanted to fly over the Earth, cleaning up all the pollution, and planting more trees."

Melanie is a grown-up green angel now. An impassioned, make-no-apologies defender of Mother Earth. The kind of person who rides her bike everywhere (despite having been struck by a car), loves vegan restaurants, always carries a mug and plate, conserves paper, and never, ever uses plastic bags.

But Melanie's green gusto goes way, way beyond that. She has a degree in environmental engineering. She travels to environmental conferences all over the planet. She was a political candidate and deputy leader of the Green Party of Ontario. And she already has a big collection of awards.

> ❝ 'To feel like you're a part of this huge change that can happen and this huge opportunity that's been given to our generation is something a lot of young people are recognizing," says 26-year-old Melanie. "I think it's a defining cause because we have such opportunity right now to make that link and move forward.' ❞

73

No, there's nothing subtle about Melanie Mullen's mission. She's fully committed to her journey toward a healthier planet. And she's in it for life. "To feel like you're a part of this huge change that can happen and this huge opportunity that's been given to our generation is something a lot of young people are recognizing," says 26-year-old Melanie. "I think it's a defining cause because we have such opportunity right now to make that link and move forward."

Melanie's green passions grew out of her family's green thumbs. The year she was born, her parents opened the Mullen Garden Market in Niagara Falls. Melanie's childhood was a happy mishmash of mulch, manure, and marigolds. "There's pictures of me, like, three years old with the hose, just going up and down watering the flowers," she says. "And shoveling the manure."

As Melanie got older, she learned the environment wasn't all roses and rain. She started hearing about pollution and other bad things humans were doing to the Earth. "That was like a turning point," she says. "I realized that pollution existed, and we were the reason why it existed, and we were the ones who were just spreading it like wildfire."

That realization lit a fire in young Melanie's soul, turning her into a pint-sized crusader for the planet. She started an environmental club at her school when she was just 10 years old. In grade eight, she wrote a poem about pollution, had it printed on T-shirts, and sold them to raise money to save the rainforest. By the time she was in high school, she was protesting at the

provincial legislature and promoting recycling at her school. She even won an environmental award from the city.

From the beginning of her activism, Melanie believed she had a responsibility to do something for the Earth. "I think it's because I was always taught to count my blessings before I go to bed," she says. "I remember before I'd fall asleep, I'd almost come to tears because I felt so lucky to have a nice family. I always felt so blessed, and out of that blessing came responsibility. I felt really obligated to take that blessing and put it into action and do something good."

And so, Melanie's determination kept growing. After graduating from high school, she looked for university programs that included the word "environment." Eventually, she found her way into the environmental engineering program at the University of Guelph. Even with the pressure of her studies, Melanie found time for on-campus activism. She hosted an environmental radio show for four years, organized a "Buy Nothing Day," and helped run a "Lug-A-Mug" campaign. Once, she and some friends collected all the Styrofoam cups they could find on campus and turned them into a giant, garish snake. As Melanie says, her brand of activism always had a "creative twist."

But even with her brash, sometimes theatrical style of protest, no one expected what came next. The year Melanie graduated from university, she threw her green hat into the political ring.

She ran in the Ontario provincial election as a candidate for — you guessed it — the Green Party. "I didn't really decide to do it," says Melanie, who was 24 at the time of the election. "I just did it. And it shocked my family. It shocked everybody. Because none of us ever thought of politics as something that's attractive or something you would want to be a part of."

Melanie ran against two seasoned, middle-aged male politicians. She had grown up seeing them in the news. And then, suddenly, she was in the picture. "It was challenging on the politics side," she says. "The arguing and the debating, and the attacking, or the political game. So initially, I got a little bit overwhelmed with that. Then I just realized I'm not a politician. I'm not a seasoned politician. I have no experience with this. I'm just going to fulfill what I do have experience with, and that's sharing these ideas and opening new avenues of thought."

Melanie campaigned with all her might, shaking hands, doing interviews, and speaking on TV. She talked about the need for renewable energy, better public transit, and smarter use of land. But despite her hard work, she came in third on election night. It wasn't all disappointment, though. With more than 11 percent of the vote, she had the satisfaction of knowing that many people were mulling over the Mullen message. "Going door to door, people were open to talking about new ideas, new approaches," she says. "They wanted to learn how to be green. I am so happy with that. That

showed that everybody was green inside. They are green inside and want to vote Green."

Weeks after the election, Melanie represented the Green Party of Canada at the United Nations Framework Convention on Climate Change in Bali, Indonesia. She was then named deputy leader of the Green Party of Ontario. She even went to Brazil for a gathering of the Global Greens, an international network of Green parties and political movements. "I have been fortunate," she says, "to meet and consult with many Green leaders from around the world."

More recently, Melanie won praise for making a big splash in downtown Niagara Falls. She and two other young people started a non-profit organization called Celebrate Old Downtown. Their goal was to rejuvenate the historic Queen Street area. "As soon as the malls showed up, the downtown started falling apart," she says. "So all these local businesses kind of were drowned out and the economies took a spin. It really drains the quality of life."

Melanie had planned to spend three years working with Celebrate Old Downtown. But she reached her goals in just one year. An old theatre is being restored. New restaurants and art galleries are opening. And Queen Street is alive with festivals and other big events. "The downtown is on a sustainable path to full revitalization and full economic and green stability," Melanie says. "The new small business owners are all on board, so I let them take it from here!"

As a young woman breathing life into the old downtown, Melanie impressed a lot of people. An artist named Sarah Marie Lacy met Melanie at a Saturday art festival on Queen Street. She felt inspired to write about the experience in her blog, describing Melanie as bubbly, enthusiastic, and passionate. "Everyone says they want to change the world," Sarah wrote. "She is actually doing just that. She literally is 'being the change she wants to see in the world.' It's people like her who are going to save this planet, because she is going to inspire the rest of us plebs to actually do something too. I'll definitely be keeping an eye out for her, because this is a woman who is going places."

Melanie was presented with a Good Canadian Citizen award in Niagara Falls for her work with Celebrate Old Downtown. She has also won plenty of other honors for her activism, including an environmental youth achievement award from the Sierra Club.

So what's next for this green warrior? "I am planning something big, but can't let it out of the bag just yet," Melanie says. "But I will tell you it involves creativity and a new global green environment."

Whatever she's up to, this green angel is definitely earning her wings.

A Budding Career

Vying for Votes

LISE RICHARD, *Activist & Political Organizer*

AGE: 24

ECO-JOB: Green Party Organizer in Nova Scotia

A VOTE FOR GREEN: During the 2008 Canadian federal election campaign, Lise walked around the St. Francis Xavier University campus trying to drum up support for the Green Party and its leader, Elizabeth May.

ROOTS: When she was growing up in Dartmouth, Nova Scotia, Lise's family always recycled and composted. "I grew up with it," she says. "And it felt odd to me when I went places where people didn't recycle every bit of plastic or all their cans."

ECO-ED: She studied nutrition but wasn't passionate about it. Finally, she realized she wanted an environmental career, and she transferred into an environmental science program at St. Francis Xavier University. "It was awesome. It was tough, but it was very interesting." Lise and a friend created the Environmental Science Society on campus. The society brought in guest speakers, held retreats and a large conference, and educated faculty and students about climate change issues.

GREEN ENERGY: From the start, Lise's passion for saving the planet has had no limits. "It gave me the drive to be able to stay up for 16 hours a day and do my schoolwork and run 40 different events a year. It made me feel really good."

GLOBE-TROTTING: Lise was part of the Canadian Youth Delegation at the United Nations Framework Convention on Climate Change in Bali, Indonesia. She says she met amazing young people at the conference, but she was upset and embarrassed by Canada's contribution. More recently, Lise went to a similar UN conference in Poland.

GREEN GOALS: Lise wants to open a "completely sustainable" restaurant one day. She's also thinking about running environmental camps for young people.

ECO-ADVICE: Lise says the environmental movement is growing and needs new people. She recommends starting out by volunteering with Earth-loving organizations. "Throw caution to the wind and just do it," she says.

FAVORITE QUOTE: "Spread love everywhere you go … Let no one ever come to you without leaving better or happier." – Mother Teresa

All Aboard the Election Train!

CAMILLE LABCHUK, Public Relations Rep

Apart from the children of *Playboy* bunnies, not too many young people can say their mothers have posed naked.

But Camille Labchuk knows what it's like. Back when she was in grade nine in Prince Edward Island, Canada, Camille's mother appeared in the buff for a book that was seen around the world. In the shot, Sharon Labchuk has a black gas mask over her face. She's sitting cross-legged on fluffy red farmland, a mane of brown hair draped over her breasts.

The photograph, far from being cheap, was a bold, bare form of protest against the use of pesticides on farms. Sharon was —

and still is — one of the best-known environmental activists in Prince Edward Island.

"I remember being a bit concerned what my classmates might think, and I did get quite a few comments," says Camille, who's now 24. "These types of comments never really bothered me at that age. I always knew my mother was doing the right thing. I am a huge fan of tactics that shock people out of complacency."

For Camille, life at home was intensely, happily green. "It was always about what we could do to make our lifestyle as low-impact as possible on the planet," she says. "We always had a composter or two in the backyard. We always recycled before it was cool to do so. We lived simply. We didn't spend extravagantly. We weren't über-consumers like some families today."

Camille respected her mother's environmental work. But she didn't see herself following in those activist footsteps. In fact, Camille earned a degree in psychology. When she was in university, though, she started having second thoughts about her career choice. Studying people's brains somehow lost its allure. The green magnet was impossible to resist. "I just realized there was a part of me that was developed thanks to my activist mother that I couldn't deny anymore," Camille says. "I knew I had to do something else to be involved in the environment."

> **... not too many young people can say their mothers have posed naked.**

> **Camille didn't tiptoe into activism. She took a daring, devil-may-care dive, joining the Green Party of Canada and going as far as to run for a seat in Parliament when she was barely out of her teens.**

81

Camille didn't tiptoe into activism. She took a daring, devil-may-care dive, joining the Green Party of Canada and going as far as to run for a seat in Parliament when she was barely out of her teens. She lost the election. But when it came to green politics, she was hooked. "In the halls of Parliament and the provincial legislatures, that's really where the decisions are made. Environmentalism and activism can pressure politicians to make decisions, but it's really up to the politicians to decide how we will proceed. So I feel that my time is best spent working in this arena."

After that election, Camille spent a couple of years in Ottawa, Canada's capital city, working as a press secretary for the Green Party. She had plans to go to law school. But when she found out another federal election was coming up in 2008, she decided to stay on Parliament Hill for the campaign whirlwind. "It was fantastic," says Camille, who was swamped issuing news releases and handling media requests during the election build-up. "I am really, really pleased that I stuck around for the election. I got a lot of interesting experience."

The Green Party has been in Canada for more than 20 years, but competing with the bigger parties for national attention — and seats in Parliament — is a big challenge. The Green Party leader, Elizabeth May, wasn't even invited to take part in national TV debates for party leaders. The jilted Greens spoke out in protest, and the media was all over the controversy. In the end, the decision was reversed. "During that time it was very stressful, and it was very busy," Camille says. "But it was also pretty

exhilarating to be in the center of all of this and to actually accomplish something that we had set out to achieve, which was propelling our leader to the debate."

During the campaign, Camille's Green job even took her on a cross-country political odyssey. While other party leaders were jetting all over Canada, Elizabeth May and her supporters chose a fittingly eco-friendly option: They took the train. "We traveled on a cross-country whistle stop from Vancouver to the east coast," Camille says. "So that was very exciting. It was something unlike anything the Green Party had ever done."

The party rented an entire train car for the trip. And as they chugged their way across the world's second-largest country, they had rally after rally with supporters from Pacific to Atlantic. "We were operating on the train schedule, so we'd hop out and set up our displays," Camille says. "The leader would get off the train and talk for a couple of minutes. Then we'd have to hop back on the train literally five minutes later. And then continue on to the next stop."

In the end, the Green Party didn't win a single seat. But Camille wasn't too deflated. "One thing we've seen is the explosion of the environment as an issue for Canadians," she says. "I don't attribute that completely to our presence. But I think that by attracting a chunk of the electorate who cares about  those issues and holding that support, we've forced the other parties to green themselves up in order to attract that support back. They haven't been successful in doing that so far. And I count that as one of our successes."

Politics and Parliament aren't Camille's only passions. She's just as committed to working for wildlife. Not long after the election, she started doing public relations for the Humane Society International. The organization speaks out against the seal hunt on Canada's east coast, puppy mills, and other issues. "As long as I can remember I have been an animal lover," she says. "As a child, we had pets, and images of the seal hunt on TV deeply disturbed me. I became a vegetarian when I was 12 years old. It just kind of spiraled from there, and I got more and more involved in those issues."

A couple of years ago, Camille had the chance to take a helicopter ride to pack ice off Nova Scotia. "It was the best day

of my life," she says. "As we spiraled closer and closer to the ice, you could see little black dots. They became clearer and clearer as we got closer, and they were little baby seals. We met about five or six of them. They were curious of us, also a little wary. They hadn't experienced humans before, so they didn't really know fear of us yet. We took some photos and observed them play for a while. It was pretty incredible."

As Camille sees it, the environment is a unifying force for today's young people. "For the first time, the generation is seeing the effects of environmental degradation," she says. "We're seeing new species extinctions every day. We're hearing news of icecaps melting. And we're seeing how much the Arctic sea ice has diminished. I think being able to see the effects firsthand has really motivated a lot of people to want to do something about it."

And Camille is setting out to do a lot more for the Earth. Law school is next in her plans, and she wants to specialize, naturally, in environmental law. She says her goals as a lawyer will be advocating for animals, detoxifying the environment, and standing up for many other causes. "If you can save one block of forest from being lost, or if you can prevent one oil spill from happening, or ban one toxic chemical, maybe it will all be worthwhile," she says. "I think that there are victories to be had along the way. And if you can make a difference for some animals, some plants, some trees, or for the ocean, then you'd be silly not to take the chance."

And that, for Camille Labchuk, is the naked truth.

A Budding Career

Governmental Green
ALEXA PAGEL, *Education & Outreach Advisor*

AGE: 25

ECO-CAREER: After earning a geography degree from the University of Toronto, Alexa was hired as a research analyst with the Ministry of the Environment (MOE) in Ontario, Canada. She's since become an education and outreach advisor who promotes safe drinking water.

GREENSPIRATIONS: She grew up in a small rural community with a king-sized name. The Township of King has fewer than 20,000 people. As a child, Alexa enjoyed backyard bugs, fishing, huge fields, and the changing colors of the leaves.

GREEN GENES: Both of Alexa's parents have degrees in microbiology.

TEEN GREEN: As part of her job with the environment ministry, Alexa worked with young people, helping them develop their interest in the environment and science. "It's great," she says. "I love seeing the enthusiasm of the students."

CITIES IN BLOOM: Alexa has a passion for greening up cities. Her department held a forum on "living walls," which are walls of vegetation designed for urban spaces. She says natural beauty in the city is aesthetically appealing and serene. On top of that, it can help clean the air. (To see the leafy green work of Canadian companies, check out Nedlaw Living Walls at www.naturaire.com and Green Roofs for Healthy Cities at www.greenroofs.org).

COOL SITE: The Ontario Ministry of the Environment runs www.obviously.ca, a site loaded with info on all things green, including jobs, schools, and profiles of young environmental heroes.

EARTHY GOALS: "For career goals, they're sort of up in the air right now," Alexa says, "but corporate social responsibility for the environment looks like an exciting new area."

ECO ADVICE: For teens considering green careers, Alexa recommends getting involved with local organizations. You could, for example, work on fundraisers for environmental charities. "And this will sound silly," she says, "but read everything."

Chapter 5

SUB
SAHARAN

The Light of the Jungle

DARIO MERLO, Project Coordinator, Jane Goodall Institute (JGI)

On one of the darkest days of his childhood, an 11-year-old boy named Dario Merlo clung to his mother at an airport in the African country of Zaire. Sad and scared, he got on a plane bound for Belgium. His mother stayed behind. He didn't know if he would ever see her again.

> 'I was living by the lake, and in the lake you could see many people killed. So it was kind of a nightmare at this time. This period of life was a mess.'

"It was quite depressing," says Dario. "I was afraid that my dad and my mom would be killed. This was a real frustration. When I left, my heart was just feeling really bad."

It was a tragic turn in Dario's life. When he was younger, growing up in the city of Goma was like being in paradise. Dario and his family lived on a huge farm with thousands of cows and hundreds of horses. He'd spend weekends going to parks and looking at the wild animals. His parents taught him to love nature.

Then, in April 1994, paradise went dark. A horrific genocide was raging in the neighboring country of Rwanda. Anguish seeped across the border into Zaire — and into Dario's life. Hundreds of thousands of Rwandan refugees came to Goma, many of them dying of cholera, dysentery, and other diseases. There were bodies in the streets, and there was violence in refugee camps. The beautiful Lake Kivu, which straddles the border of Rwanda and Zaire, turned into waters of death.

"The situation was really bad," recalls Dario, now in his mid-twenties. "I was living by the lake, and in the lake you could see many people killed. So it was kind of a nightmare at this time. This period of life was a mess."

Dario's parents decided to put him on that plane and send him to Brussels, where his older brother and sister were already studying. "Don't be sad," his father said before Dario flew away. "Go to Europe, take all the knowledge they have, and then come back and bring it to your country."

Dario never forgot those words. His father's message gave him a purpose in life, and surviving the struggles gave him strength. Through 11 years of living, studying, and working in Belgium, Dario always knew he would go home to Africa. "Every day I spent (in Europe), the only reason I was able to do things fast, to study pretty fast and to do things properly, was because I was thinking about coming back to my country," he says. "I had this feeling that it was a kind of mission. And that was clear from the beginning."

And so, after earning a university degree and teaching high school in Belgium, Dario finally went back to his country at the end of 2004. By then, it was a much different place. Zaire had become the Democratic Republic of Congo (DRC). The country was reeling from the Second Congo War, which left almost four million people dead between 1998 and 2003. (Although other wars get more attention in the West, this was one of the deadliest conflicts of the last 100 years.) Every month, tens of thousands of people were still dying because of disease, starvation, and

> 'In my heart, I was really emotional at this time," he recalls. "I had the feeling that I came from so far. And I can bring electricity, light, in the middle of nowhere, where it is needed. So that was a really emotional moment for me.'

violence. And to make things even worse, a fiery eruption of the Mount Nyiragongo volcano in early 2002 had destroyed much of Goma.

"Things were really complex," recalls Dario, who is fortunate to still have both of his parents. "There were a lot of degradations in education and health. Politics was really bad, and it's still bad despite the election that happened a few years ago. ...I was happy to be back. I was feeling that there were a lot of things to do. But at the same time, I was really worried about the ability of the actual people to change anything in this area."

Dario's first challenge was to figure out what he could do to help his country. For a while, he worked with his father, building roads in the countryside, setting up a cheese factory, and training farmers. But when rebels kept destroying farms, Dario decided to find another way of making a difference. He looked at the many non-governmental organizations operating out of Goma, and one captured his attention. "I knew the Jane Goodall Institute was doing some work in the forest and things like that," he says. "They were looking for a socio-economic development manager. So I went to their office, I left my curriculum [vitae], and after that I was recruited."

Jane Goodall is a British scientist who became famous in the 1960s for her groundbreaking chimpanzee research in Africa. The Jane Goodall Institute (JGI) is dedicated to primate research

and habitat conservation. JGI works extensively in the Democratic Republic of Congo (DRC), which has more gorillas and chimpanzees than just about any other country in the world. The DRC is also the only place where endangered, chimp-like bonobos live in the wild.

When Dario started his job with JGI, his big task was to bring light to Kasugho, a remote village in the eastern part of his country. The people had barely any electricity, so they were destroying trees for firewood, thereby threatening the habitat of apes and other animals. Water was being polluted, health centers and businesses were hungry for electricity, and thieves were sneaking around in the blackness of night. Besides that, students at a university called the Tayna Center for Conservation Biology were having trouble studying. "They needed 24-hour

FOR THE LOVE OF CHIMPS

It all started with a little British girl named Jane and Jubilee, her toy chimpanzee. As she grew, Jane dreamed about living in Africa and watching and writing about animals. Finally, in 1960, the dream came true. Jane arrived at the Gombe Stream Chimpanzee Reserve in western Tanzania. It took a while, but the chimps accepted her presence. And as the months passed, she saw them hunting for meat and even making simple tools. Jane gave the chimps names, like David Greybeard and Goliath, even though some scholars criticized her for being unscientific. Jane's groundbreaking work made her famous around the globe. She received a Ph.D. in the study of animal behavior in 1965. And in 1977, she founded the Jane Goodall Institute for Wildlife Research, Education and Conservation. Now in her 70s, Jane Goodall is a Dame of the British Empire and one of the most respected environmental activists in the world.[1]

www.janegoodall.com

electricity to be able to go on the Internet and to study during the night," Dario says. "They were using a generator, which was really bad."

The savior in the forest of Kasugho was hydropower. Village leaders worked with JGI for more than two years to plan and build a 35-kilowatt hydroelectric plant. More than 200 villagers, energized by the prospect of seeing the light, volunteered to help with the construction. "It was clear that what they could do was to bring some sand, and to help to carry the equipment, the cement bags, the stones, and all of the construction materials," Dario says. "So that's what they did. They really helped in building this micro-hydro plant."

❝ His goal is to help Congolese kids understand the value of their natural resources. ❞

On a November night, the power plant lit up the night sky for the first time, transforming the lives of the 16,000 people living in the area. Dario says it was one of the best moments he has had since moving back to the DRC. "In my heart, I was really emotional at this time," he recalls. "I had the feeling that I came from so far. And I can bring electricity, light, in the middle of nowhere, where it is needed. So that was a really emotional moment for me."

It's an electric revolution for Kasugho. The future conservationists studying at the Tayna Center now have 24-hour-a-day electricity. So do a maternity center, the town center, and many mills and shops. The people also have street lamps, making their community safer. "For the population, you can easily imagine that they were really glad to have this kind of project and see that electricity is lighting their roads," Dario says. "At the university side, they were really excited to have 24-hour electricity, so they can go on the Internet, they can have light in their bedrooms, and things like that."

One of the other joys of Dario's job is meeting groups of children. In Belgium, he was a history teacher. In the DRC, he sees himself as a kind of environment teacher. His goal is to help Congolese kids understand the value of their natural resources. "Everything starts from knowledge," Dario says. "When you start with them when they are young, you have people that will be adults. They will make decisions tomorrow in their villages, and in their country. So it's really exciting to talk with little children and help involve them in nature conservation."

Dario has seen horrors that most young people around the world can't imagine. His country is still in crisis, and there is suffering everywhere. Yet he is full of hope, focusing on the remarkable strength of the Congolese people. "My dad and my mom struggled so much to teach us that even when things are destroyed, even when things go wrong, you can always build something," Dario says. "You can always start something. I can tell you that despite all the fights, all the political problems, the people in this country are so dynamic and ready for change. They really need just some leaders to do something great."

The sad little boy on the airplane has grown into one of those inspiring leaders, bringing a light of hope into the darkness of the Congo.

CHARITY: WATER

Scott Harrison used to make a living as a nightclub promoter in New York City. Desperately unhappy and facing "spiritual bankruptcy," he signed up as a volunteer aboard a floating hospital with an organization called Mercy Ships (www.mercyships.org). The poverty he saw in Africa affected him so deeply he went on to found *charity: water*, a not-for-profit group on a mission to bring clean, safe drinking water to people in developing countries.[2] Find out more at www.charitywater.org.

Kuku for Kenya

MEGHAN BAILEY, Natural Resources Specialist

On a sweltering sub-Saharan day, Feathers the chicken was probably the luckiest little "kuku" in Kenya.

A tree farmer from a tiny village decided the clucker would be the perfect way to say thank you to a special person. She wrapped a strip of fabric around his gnarled claws, smoothed his gold-and-brown feathers, and placed the bird in the hands of a young, blond Canadian known as Megi-Kadzo. Although Feathers didn't know it, this Megi, with her silver nose ring and smiling blue eyes, was straight out of a chicken's dream.

Yes, Megi was a vegetarian.

And so, she saved the chicken from the spit, kept him as a pet, and gave him his fluffy name. Chicken and Canadian became a great pair, sharing everything and going places together. The frisky fowl escaped from his pen from time to time, but someone always found him and brought him back home to Megi. "Habare? Habare ya kuku?" the locals would call in Swahili as Megi walked or rode her motorbike around the town of Mariakani. "How are you? How is your chicken?"

"One time I was trying to make a deadline," says 23-year-old Megi, whose real name is Meghan Bailey. "So when Feathers was brought to my office, I had to keep him on my lap as I typed on my laptop. He seemed pretty pleased with himself. A month or so ago, though, Feathers wandered off and was not found. I think it's probably because at that point he was big enough for a feast."

The gift chicken, wherever he is, was a symbol of what Meghan has come to mean to many people in rural Kenya. Her unofficial new African name reveals just as much affection. Kadzo means "beautiful one" in Kigiriama, a local language. (Many Kenyans find the name "Meghan" too hard to pronounce.) Meghan has devoted herself to making a difference in the lives of poor people in the East African country. She works as a natural resources specialist with Aga Khan Foundation Canada, a non-profit agency that supports social development programs in Africa and Asia. In this ultimate eco-job, Meghan works closely with rural families in running a host of experimental tree farms.

THE WATER CRISIS

Here's something to think about the next time you turn on the tap for a glass of water. According to the United Nations, 1.1-billion people don't have access to clean water. That's 18 percent of the population of the planet. Things are so urgent the U.N. has proclaimed 2005 - 2015 the "Water for Life" decade.[3]
www.un.org/waterforlifedecade

"I get up early, usually around 6:00 a.m.," says Meghan, who lives in the city of Mombasa and travels 25 miles (40 kilometers) to Mariakani every day in a "matatu," a rundown minibus. "It's much more comfortable to work before the sun peaks. At the moment, planting season is in full swing, so I spend my entire day on a motorbike. I am currently working in about 20 villages, setting up demonstration tree farms. So I spend a lot of time on the road."

So why the focus on trees? Deforestation is a huge problem in Kenya. Less than two percent of the land is covered with trees, and things are getting worse. "Between 1990 and 2005 alone, the country lost 500,000 acres of its indigenous forests," says Meghan, who earned a degree in public affairs and policy management back in Canada. "People are forced to harvest the trees around them in order to satisfy their household energy, and in doing so they completely deforest their surrounding areas and contribute to all kinds of environmental effects. Erosion is the biggest one. It also makes the place a lot less aesthetic, and there's less shade. ... The hardest part is that it makes their soil very nutrient deficient. It makes it much more difficult to sustain themselves off the crops that they produce."

While the Western world relies on gas and oil, Kenyans use firewood and wood charcoal as their main fuels. Much of

96

(continued on page 97)

MEET THE ECO-PIONEERS

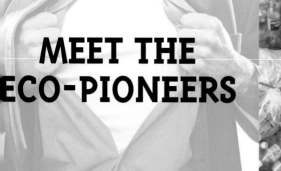

Tom Szaky (p. 16)
CEO, TerraCycle
Photo courtesy of TerraCycle, Inc.

Maia Green (p. 22)
Director, FUN (Friends Uniting For Nature) Camps

Tree Sturman (p. 36)
Horticulturalist,
Chicago Botanic Garden
Photo by Robin Carlson

Robert Niven (p. 29)
President, Carbon Sense Solutions, Inc.

Julian Mocine-McQueen (p. 45)
Field Organizer, Green For All

Markese Bryant (p. 49)
Musician & Green Entrepreneur

Erica Stolp (p. 55)
Environmental Technician

Matt Lee (p. 50)
Urban Planning Student
Photo by Eric Chan

Rebecca Bruce (p. 64)
Sustainable Architect

Stet Sanborn (p. 59)
Architect

Josh Kjenner (p. 70)
Mechanical Engineer

Melanie Mullen (p. 73)
Activist & Political Candidate

Lise Richard (p. 79)
Activist & Political Organizer

ON'T COOK THE CLIMATE !

Camille Labchuk (p. 80)
Public Relations Rep

Dario Merlo (p. 88)
Project Coordinator, Jane Goodall Institute (JGI)
Photo courtesy of the Jane Goodall Institute

Meghan Bailey (p. 94)
Natural Resources Specialist

Alexa Pagel (p. 85)
Education & Outreach Advisor
Photo by Jason Williams

Daniel Musgrave (p. 104)
Bonobo Caretaker & Research Assistant
Photo courtesy of Great Ape Trust of Iowa

Sonja Eisfeld (p. 114), *using a hydrophone*
Marine Biologist
Photo by Simon Keith

Nathan, The Bonobo Ape (p. 107)
Photo courtesy of Great Ape Trust of Iowa

Lindsay Collins (p. 121)
Outdoor Adventure Guide

Zoë Bradbury (p. 127)
Organic Farmer
Photo by Daniel DeSurra

Tom Garvey (p. 134)
Brewer
Photo by Adam W. King

Julia Clark (p. 139)
Program Associate,
Scientific Certification Systems

Andrew Walsh (p. 142)
Environmental Health Practitioner

Nneka Leiba (p. 148)
Environmental Health Researcher
Photo courtesy of Environmental Working Group

Sarah Lesperance (p. 154)
Physician

Nicole Cabana (p. 166)
Pilot
Photo courtesy of NOAA AOC

Rosa Kouri (p. 174)
Environmental Activist

Alexandra Jahn (p. 161), *in front of the CCGS Amundsen.*
Meteorologist

Caroline Lee (p. 183)
Resource & Environmental
Management Graduate Student

Genevieve Gilbert (p. 188)
Climate Change Adaptation Graduate Student

Caustan De Riggs (p. 197)
Entertainer, Entrepreneur & Activist
Photo by David Smith, Lifetouch

Soyeon Lee (p. 205),
shown to the right, wearing her famous juice box gown.
Classical Pianist
Photos courtesy of Soyeon Lee

Jennifer Cummings (p. 191)
Eco-Fashion Designer

(continued from page 96)

the cutting of old forests is against the law, but it keeps happening. And many poor people, desperate to find ways to survive, cut indigenous trees as a last-ditch way of making money. "Communities are left trapped in a dangerous cycle as poverty and environmental degradation perpetuate each other," Meghan says. "They destroy their most important resource in an effort to stay alive."

Meghan sees tragic poverty all the time. Frequent droughts ravage farms in the countryside around Mariakani, and deforestation is turning much of the fertile land into desert. At the same time, food prices are skyrocketing, leaving many families desperately hungry. In some areas, three-quarters of the children are malnourished, and many die before reaching their fifth birthdays. Sometimes, food runs out before the next growing season can begin, and that painful gap can last up to two months. "When this happens, food is strictly rationed as the supply nears the end," Meghan says. "Children may only eat watered-down porridge each day until the next harvest."

> **'I truly feel that the program I am running will have substantial, long-lasting, positive impacts for the farmers involved. I feel great joy being able to facilitate that.'**

Aga Khan Foundation and a Kenyan organization called KOMAZA work together to run the tree-growing program. Through it, Meghan plants not only trees, but hope. Her goal is to turn wastelands into well-managed tree farms that will become an important, life-changing source of income for Kenyan families. The seedlings being planted today have the potential to grow into a sustainable supply of charcoal and

lumber. Eventually, the farmers should be able to sell the wood and feed their families. At least some indigenous trees would be saved. And the forests would have the chance to start flourishing again.

"I love working with farmers," Meghan says. "It's by far the most enjoyable part of my job. I get to spend a lot of time at individual homesteads. ... I truly feel that the program I am running will have substantial, long-lasting, positive impacts for the farmers involved. I feel great joy being able to facilitate that. Being able to plant trees on wasteland that can't be used to grow anything else is, I think, a great success — at least for the farmers who own the land."

WASTE IN THE WEST

While so many people in the world are hungry and struggling to survive, Western nations continue to waste food. According to Statistics Canada, an estimated 38 percent of solid food available for retail sale was wasted in 2007. That's the equivalent of 403.45 pounds (183 kilograms) per person.[4]

Meghan comes from a part of the world where 80 percent of the land is forested. She grew up in the province of New Brunswick on Canada's east coast. Although her parents didn't work in Africa or fight for environmental causes, they helped inspire her green direction in life. "My mother is a social worker, so we always grew up with the idea that we should effect change on our surroundings," she says. "My parents were very adamant that we recycle everything. Other than that I wouldn't necessarily say that they're environmentalists. But certainly the idea that we should effect change was completely instilled in us."

As a girl, Meghan found herself moved by TV images of starving children in Africa. And by the time she was in the middle of her degree, she was offered a chance to spend a year studying at the University of Ghana. "I don't even know if I really, really wanted to go," she recalls. "I just thought it would be a good experience. But when I got there, I realized it would be a good fit for me."

Such a good fit, in fact, that Meghan couldn't pass up the chance to go to Kenya with Aga Khan Foundation Canada. After just a few months on the job, she was offered the chance to stay for a year. "The extended contract has meant that I can now really settle in to life here," she says, "which is great because I'm here for the long haul!"

Of course, settling into a new life in Kenya means surviving some transcontinental culture shock. The smog of Mombasa can be sickly. People burn garbage in their driveways. And a Westerner like Meghan always gets stares. "You can't really go anywhere without getting a lot of attention," Meghan says. "People associate you as a foreigner with all kinds of things, good and bad. So it can be difficult to have a social life. You have to be very careful of the way you word things so as not to offend people. I've stomached a bit of meat because I didn't want to offend people when they offered me food in their home."

Communication can also be a huge challenge. The Kenyan farmers speak two local dialects, but they also speak Swahili. "I do speak some Swahili," Meghan says. "On certain topics my

vocabulary is better than others. For large community meetings, I still prefer to use a translator. But for one-on-one interactions I can usually get by OK. I'm learning as I go and hope to be fluent within the year. That was my resolution this year!"

Working in rural Africa means the occasional chicken on your lap — or monkey on your back. Since the mysterious disappearance of Feathers, Meghan has cared for a few other critters. One tree farmer found a baby monkey whose mother had been killed by a dog, and Meghan took care of the furry orphan. "I brought it to a wildlife sanctuary, but in the meantime it was living in my

house for a couple of days," she says. "It didn't like being alone, so it would just cling to my shirt. It held itself up, so I could more-or-less go about my normal business for the day. Random stuff like that happens all the time. There is never a dull day."

For Meghan, one of the big rewards of the job is seeing how much the tree farming means to families. Some have tree nurseries, and lovingly tend to their tiny seedlings. Another family worked just as hard on an experimental tree plot. "It was just a small plot to see if the trees could grow in an area with less fertile soil and very low rainfall," Meghan says. "To monitor growth, I used to visit their farm and home quite often. They were very pleased to have been chosen to run the farm. They took such pride in it that they even decorated the thorn fence protecting the young trees with beautiful seashells. They gave me Feathers to thank me for planting the farm with them."

But in the face of Kenya's shattering poverty and hunger, Meghan admits she has questioned whether she should be asking people to plant trees. Not long ago, someone took away those doubts. It was a woman with a baby boy strapped to her back. "She runs one of my tree farms as an income-generating activity," Meghan says. "We were chatting about food prices, and she was sharing some of her ingenious tricks on how to spread out the food so it lasts longer. When I complimented her on her resourcefulness, she smiled and said it was fine for now. But for the baby, trees were her plan."

Meghan inspires people in Kenya — and at home. Her younger sister Kristy is studying wildlife rehabilitation and would like to work in Africa someday. "Meghan has found the perfect place to fulfill her desire to help individuals, communities, and the environment," Kristy says. "She has never chosen a predictable path in life, and I wouldn't expect anything less incredible from her than what she is doing now. Meghan has inspired me to look for change and not accept the status quo. Her passion for helping others has motivated me to seek meaningful, fulfilling experiences. She encouraged me to take the road less traveled, and the experiences are the reward."

Meghan loves going home to New Brunswick to visit her family. And she says she may go back to North America to earn a master's degree one day. But for now, her dreams and ambitions are in the shape of Africa. "I feel very satisfied by what I'm doing

now," she says. "I imagine I'll stay in sub-Saharan Africa working on community-based natural resource management projects for the foreseeable future. At this point, the farthest I look ahead is usually the next rainy season! But I hope that over time I'll build an expertise that I can lend to other organizations or individuals that are doing good work. Maybe I'll write a book on it."

So it could be a while before the Kenyan people, who are finding such hope in seedlings, have to say good-bye to their Megi-Kadzo.

Chapter 6

WILD
THINGS

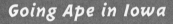

Going Ape in Iowa

DANIEL MUSGRAVE, Bonobo Caretaker & Research Assistant

The girls are wild about Daniel Musgrave. And he knows it.

They love to take his hand, hug him, and blow kisses his way. They can't get enough of his singing, especially when he breaks into Beatles tunes like "Hard Day's Night" or the '80s hit "Jukebox Hero."

When they're feeling really affectionate, they even pick dirt from under his nails or run their fingers through his curly brown hair. "Any hairs that look out of place they'll kind of pluck," Daniel says. "It feels really good. It's like a massage."

> **"** 'The idea of inter-species communication, the ability to get into another species' mind, at least at some level, was just beyond belief for me," says Daniel, who's 25. "I had to see what it was like.' **"**

Daniel spends his workdays, his birthdays, and even some Christmas Days hanging out with these girls — and a few guys too. He just can't get enough of Kanzi, Panbanisha, Elikya, Maisha, Matata, Nathan, and Nyota, the seven stupendous bonobo apes of Great Ape Trust of Iowa.

"I consider them like a second family," he says. "I know that sounds kind of funny. But I appreciate every moment. I try to make the most of all of it."

Great Ape Trust was built a few years ago on 200 acres of lowlands, forests, and lakes not far from Des Moines. It's not a zoo, but a center for studying the intelligence and behavior of bonobos, gorillas, chimpanzees, and orangutans. Its mission includes providing

an "honorable life" for great apes, promoting their conservation, and educating the public. The apes living at the Trust come from zoos and research centers in the United States.

When Daniel saw a presentation about Great Ape Trust at his college, he knew he had to be a part of it. He wrote to the people in charge, telling them he would do anything — even clean the toilets. "The idea of inter-species communication, the ability to get into another species' mind, at least at some level, was just beyond belief for me," says Daniel, who's 25. "I had to see what it was like."

Daniel's fascination with apes started in a morbid way. As a teenager living in Kansas, he did volunteer work with a museum. Part of his job was to help prepare dead moles, bats, and other small mammals to be displayed. "But one day, we had a chimpanzee that had died at a local zoo from heart failure," Daniel recalls. "I was really weirded out. It was the hands. The hands were so close to ours that I had all sorts of ethical questions come up in my mind about what I was doing. To me, it wasn't just some animal."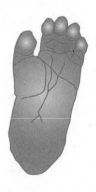

Daniel couldn't get the image of the dead chimp out of his head. Later, he thought about becoming a biologist. But when he was in college in Iowa, he realized he didn't want to spend his life studying microscopic organisms. He wanted to work with live animals.

Around that time, Daniel sent his application letter to Great Ape Trust. Before long, he was offered the chance to do volunteer work with apes. On his first day at the Trust, Daniel got to spend

a couple of minutes with the bonobos. Even though he and the apes were separated by wire mesh for safety reasons, he was thrilled. For the apes, though, it wasn't love at first sight. "They eyed me in a suspicious way," says Daniel. "For me, it was overpowering to be around them. There's a lot going on behind those eyes. And if you're not prepared for it, it just kind of stupefies you."

> ❝ ... Daniel was a kind of bonobo butler, cleaning their home and cooking up everything from burgers to burritos. ❞

Daniel didn't push the relationship. Even though he had never been around bonobos, he knew it would take time to win them over. "It was a slow process the first couple of months," he says. "I had to earn my right to be a part of the group and to interact with everybody. The bonobos had to check me out and make sure that I was OK and that I wasn't some sort of strange male just looking for trouble."

A lot of people haven't even heard of bonobos, probably because there are so few of them. Only about 10,000 to 50,000 are left in the world. (The only bonobos in the wild live in the Democratic Republic of Congo in Africa.) With their black hair, slender bodies, and wispy chin whiskers, they look like a less muscular version of the chimpanzee. In groups of bonobos, the females are equal or superior to the males. Matata is the matriarch bonobo at Great Ape Trust. She was born in the wild in Africa in 1970. Kanzi is her son, and her daughters are Panbanisha, Maisha, and Elikya. The babes of the group are Nathan and Nyota, Panbanisha's boys.

For months, Daniel was a kind of bonobo butler, cleaning their home and cooking up everything from burgers to burritos. He continued to be separated from the apes by the wire mesh. "The risk is that they move really, really fast," he explains. "And they have a lot more strength than we do, and so they're used to playing rough. They're used to bonobos being able to take a little bit more physical activity than humans can take because we're soft. We're just not built the same way. So a lot of the time it's not that they mean to hurt us. It's just that they mean to kind of give us a physical message. Whereas on a bonobo it would be like a tap on the shoulder, to us it might leave a bruise."

After four months as a volunteer, Daniel asked Great Ape Trust whether he could spend his Christmas break with the animals. "I wanted to be there as much as possible," he says.

And that's when things took off. Daniel was at the Trust almost all of the time that Christmas season. Finally, he was allowed to be in the same space as some of the bonobos. He chased and tickled the younger apes. The adult apes, who loved making loud noises and trying to show Daniel how tough they were, started to quiet down. At last, he had had won their trust and affection. He was in.

Daniel was later hired as a bonobo caretaker. And these days, he's also a research assistant at the Trust. One of his best buddies is Nathan, an eight-year-old bonobo with a passion for peppermint patties. "We hang out, and he's always very gentle with me," Daniel says. "He's always looking for special attention and alone time. We groom a lot. He lets me rub his back

and tickle him. And I never have to worry about him doing anything mischievous. Some of the other kids, they might sneak in a little bite here and there, maybe try to scare you every once in a while. And I don't have anything like that with Nathan."

The matriarch, Matata, was harder to impress. But when she saw the rapport Daniel had with her children and grandchildren, she warmed up to him too. "Bonobo girls like me," Daniel says. "I don't know what it was. But they thought I was OK. And Matata kind of called dibs on me, I guess. So she likes to take me around, and she leads me by the hand. I think she thinks that I'm kind of like a child who needs to be taught things. And she really has this kind of nurturing ability and attitude to her."

FAREWELL, NATHAN

Sadly, Nathan the bonobo died not long after Daniel Musgrave was interviewed for this book. The eight-year-old ape, who loved tickles, grapes, and stuffed animals, was the youngest bonobo living at Great Ape Trust of Iowa. He was also one of Daniel's best buds. Nathan was usually active, but he started having allergy-like symptoms. Veterinarians later discovered he had an advanced, inoperable case of lymphoma. Nathan died peacefully while under sedation.[1]

One of the most amazing things about the apes at the Trust is that they understand some human language. The apes express their thoughts and feelings to people by touching more than 300 symbols — or lexigrams — on a large computer screen. There's also a paper chart of symbols that Daniel and the other staff can carry around. "We talk about everything," Daniel says. "They can understand what I am saying almost all of the time."

In one of these ape-to-human conversations, Panbanisha touched the lexigram for the word "secret" and cupped her hand around her ear. In a whisper, Daniel asked Panbanisha what kind of secret she was thinking about. She looked him in the eyes, thought for a moment, and then went back to the computer and touched the lexigrams for "marshmallows," "quiet," and "secret." She was asking Daniel to sneak her a snack. "The reason why it's a secret," he says, "is because they're on a diet and she doesn't want other people to know that she's getting these special treats."

Kanzi, meanwhile, is a superstar among apes. He is considered the first bonobo in the world to demonstrate a real comprehension of spoken language. He can understand more than 500 words. (That's about the same as a two-and-a-half-year-old child!) Kanzi is also an accomplished tool maker, and his stone knives are sharp enough to cut through thick rope. Books have been written about him, he has been featured in *Smithsonian* magazine, and he has his own Wikipedia entry. The amazing ape has even been known to hang out with rock stars. Kanzi has jammed on his keyboard with Paul McCartney and Peter Gabriel.

BONOBO LOVE

Bonobos are a happy, sexy bunch. They live in groups, they take care of one another, and they love to share. But what they really like is, um ... getting it on. Yes, bonobos have a lot of sex. And not just the baby-making kind. Like many humans, bonobos have sex because they enjoy it. To them, a little hot stuff is a great way of getting to know someone, relaxing, or making up after a dispute.[2] Now that's wild.

But Daniel knows things the rest of the world doesn't know. Like just how much Kanzi and the other bonobos love Santa Claus. Daniel has spent his last four Christmases at the Trust. One Christmas Eve, he told the apes they had to be very good because Santa was coming with surprises. "Everybody was so happy, and they were so good, and nobody had any disagreements," Daniel recalls. "And Kanzi and Panbanisha, they demanded that we open up a door to this kind of porch area so that they could go outside. They bundled up in blankets, and they had to watch. They were watching to see when Santa was going to come. They stood guard the whole day."

The next morning, the bonobos couldn't wait to tear into their surprises. They found candy, kazoos, Play-Doh, balls, whistles, recorders, and other treats. Daniel says Christmas with the bonobos is like Christmas with children. "They're all happy, and everybody's so excited," he says. "Everybody sits there and they unwrap their presents on their own. It's really a lot of fun."

SAVING THE BONOBO

A non-profit organization called the Bonobo Conservation Initiative (BCI) is working to protect bonobos and their rainforest habitat in Africa. BCI, which is based in both Washington, D.C., and the Democratic Republic of Congo (DRC), does bonobo surveys, establishes protected areas, and tries to educate the world about the apes.[3] BCI helped create the new Kokolopori Bonobo Reserve in the DRC. The Reserve, which is larger than Rhode Island, is home to more than 1,000 bonobos.[4] You can read more about BCI and bonobos at www.bonobo.org.

Each summer, Daniel spends his birthday with the bonobos too. "I bring presents to them, not the other way around," he says. "And we all get in a space where the whole group can be

together. And I'll get cake, but everybody else gets something special too. They'll watch me blow out the candles, and there's a lot of vocalizing while we sing 'Happy Birthday.' So it's kind of like they want to sing along."

The scientists and other staff at Great Ape Trust appreciate Daniel's special rapport with the bonobos. "The bonobos have a deep affection for Daniel, and they enjoy his happy, playful approach to research and care," says Bill Fields, the Director of Scientific research. "He often sings while he works. The happiness that arises out of his perpetual song is beautiful. His abiding concern for ape welfare, conservation, and the well-being of others speaks of his character and intelligence. Daniel is a good person with a wonderful mind."

Daniel loves the day-to-day interaction with the bonobos, their hugs and kisses, and the human-ape conversations. But the job has its difficult moments. "We have disagreements," he says. "If they want something that you can't give them, or a few of the apes are getting on each other's nerves, it's tough. It just makes it harder to do daily things when people are having disagreements."

But for Daniel, the most wrenching day at the Trust was when a beloved ape passed away. P-Suke (pronounced PEACE-kay) was the 27-year-old father of Elikya, Nathan, Nyota, and Maisha. The gentle ape had spent time in a circus, and he used to be the only bonobo in Japan. At the Great Ape Trust, P-Suke

would spend hours caring for the younger bonobos while their mothers napped. In 2006, he was about to have surgery for a hernia. But when he went under anaesthesia, he died.

"For me, it was just tough," Daniel says. "I don't know how to explain it. It was not like losing an animal. It was like losing a friend. There was no distinction. There was nothing about it that made it feel any different. And for the apes, you could tell it was a big deal. Everybody was really down for the next long while. And sometimes they still talk about him. They still use his lexigram. Sometimes they'll use it when they're scared."

For Daniel, it's hard thinking about the fact that bonobos are in danger of extinction. He says he feels a little helpless, and he wishes there were something more he could do. But a few times a year, when the public is allowed to visit Great Ape Trust, he does his part to show everyone how important and special bonobos are. "We're at least trying," he says. "We are creating awareness. I mean, a lot of people don't even know what a bonobo is because they are so rare and they look so much like chimpanzees. ... We're kind of a small institution, but we're doing as much as we can. And I think that we reach quite a few people."

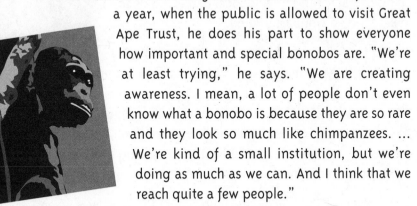

No wonder those bonobos keep the kisses coming.

GREAT APE TRUST

Great Ape Trust of Iowa does more than study apes in captivity. The Trust is on mission to advance the conservation of great apes around the world.

"Most of us feel that one can't really meaningfully work on the thinking abilities, cognitive abilities, of great apes in a captive setting without accepting some responsibility for their status in the wild," explains Dr. Benjamin Beck, the Director of Conservation with the Trust. "For the first three or four years of our existence, what we were doing is providing small grants to other organizations who were working to conserve apes in Africa and in Indonesia."

The Trust has put hundreds of thousands of dollars toward two major initiatives: The Ketambe Research Center in northern Sumatra and the Gishwati Area Conservation Program in Rwanda. The Indonesian project focuses on saving about 7,000 Sumatran orangutans, which are critically endangered. Illegal logging has destroyed much of the apes' habitat.

In Rwanda, the Gishwati Forest is home to a tiny population of chimpanzees. " The forest used to have thousands of chimpanzees, and now it has only, to the best of our counts, fourteen chimpanzees," says Dr. Beck. "This is an Alamo for chimpanzees. We've got fourteen chimpanzees in 10 square kilometers (3.86 square miles) of forest surrounded by hundreds of thousands of people, all of whom want that forest. So this is a desperate situation."

For Great Ape Trust, public education is also a part of conservation. The Trust welcomes visitors a few times each year. Dr. Beck, who has studied primates for more than 35 years, says seeing apes for the first time can be a "transformative experience" for people. "We can show the world the extraordinary cognitive abilities of great apes," he says. "As those very human-like characters emerge and become known, we would like to believe that that makes people more likely to support their conservation."

For more information about Great Ape Trust, visit www.greatapetrust.org.

A Girl Named Dave

SONJA EISFELD, Marine Biologist

This is the story of a young woman from Deutschland and her dealings with a darling dolphin named Dave.

This dolphin, unlike most Daves, was actually a girl. And for some reason, she decided to live in the waters off the town of Folkestone in England's Kent county. Dave stayed in the harbor for more than a year, splashing up a ton of excitement. Everybody had to see her. Many rushed to swim with her. Shaky amateur videos of her were posted on YouTube. Dave the bottlenose dolphin was a friendly, flippered celebrity of the sea.

> ❝'A lot of people say, 'Well, that dolphin is out there so I don't have to go to Florida to swim with them,'" Sonja says. "So they jump in the water. But they don't get the fact that it actually might harm the dolphin because the dolphin completely loses its respect and its fear of something it doesn't know.'❞

As Dave was achieving star status, Sonja Eisfeld was a young marine biologist looking for work. She decided to go to a conference of the European Cetacean Society, and she ran into the science director from the Whale and Dolphin Conservation Society (WDCS), an international charity dedicated to conserving all whales, dolphins, and porpoises. He offered her a job.

Sonja's first assignment? Dave the dolphin.

"And so I sat for six weeks," she recalls with a warm laugh. "I sat on a beach in Kent and watched this dolphin, which was brilliant. It was absolutely amazing."

Dolphins are sociable animals that live in groups, but solitary dolphins are common too. Sonja's job was to observe how Dave's behavior changed as the weeks passed. Although solitary dolphins are usually wary of humans, that can change quickly. "(People) will take boats or little dinghies or kayaks to see that dolphin," Sonja says. "The dolphin gets tamed in the end, and so it gets used to people coming towards it."

But Dave's story is no dolphin fairy tale. The experts say making friends with humans can hurt the animals. "A lot of people say, 'Well, that dolphin is out there so I don't have to go to Florida to swim with them,'" Sonja says. "So they jump in the water. But they don't get the fact that it actually might harm the dolphin because the dolphin completely loses its respect and its fear of something it doesn't know. There have been so many solitaries before, and they have all had injuries because they get too boisterous and they go near boats. They get cut by the propellers, or people cut them on purpose. It's a really, really hairy subject."

Folks all over the planet have fun-filled fantasies about swimming with dolphins, and plenty of tour companies bring in oceans of cash making those dreams come true. For the 32-year-old German-born biologist, admiring dolphins from a safe distance is good enough. "They make me quite happy when I see them," she says. "They're just amazing creatures."

Not that she always liked what she saw during the six weeks in Folkestone. Sonja says Dave had a resting place near a buoy,

but people would kayak or swim out and pester her. Some started calling Dave their "soul mate" or "best friend." They wouldn't leave the animal alone. "Do you really think that's the best idea to swim with that dolphin?" Sonja said to them. "Or is it just the best idea for you right now?"

Some of Dave's fans admitted they were being selfish. But the next day, they would be back in the water. "They see a dolphin," Sonja says, "and all common sense goes out the window."

During her six weeks on the beach, Sonja saw changes in Dave. The dolphin became more excited, jumping on top of people and trying to dunk them in the water. Dave would get in front of swimmers and cut them off from the beach. Sometimes, she stopped eating. Finally, there was trouble. "Part of her tail fluke was just gone, and it was a clean cut," Sonja says. "She had a hook embedded in her dorsal fin. So there was some entanglement in fishing gear, I think. And then she just disappeared. She was gone. And nobody knows where she went or if she's still alive."

Many years before Dave's sad saga, Sonja first heard the call of the ocean. As a twelve-year-old growing up in the countryside of western Germany, she saw a film about a girl living by the St. Lawrence River in Canada. In the movie, a marine biologist was studying dolphins and humpback whales. Sonja was inspired. "My God, this sounds so amazingly interesting," she remembers thinking at the time. "I want to do that when I grow up."

After high school, Sonja did a degree in marine biology in Germany, later enrolling in the marine mammal science program at the University of Wales. Her master's thesis focused on the social behavior of dolphins, so she spent time observing the animals from a little inflatable boat on the coast of Scotland. "It was like watching a soap opera," Sonja says, laughing. "You could see the females having calves and swimming around together, and then there would be two males working together to get a female to mate with. And it's just like a proper soap opera. It's just really, really, really cool."

Sonja had great times on the water. One day, a few dolphins were lingering around the boat. The babe of the bunch was playing. "It came towards the boat and had a jellyfish on its nose," Sonja says. "It chucked the jellyfish up next to us in the boat. And he was just chucking this jellyfish and looking over. And we were like, 'We would like to join in, but it's not allowed.' We can't jump in the water and do something like that."

When she finished her master's degree, Sonja went back to her home country and worked for the German environment ministry for more than two years. She spent most of her time in an office, writing a conservation plan for harbor porpoises in the North Sea. Less than a year after finishing that job, the WDCS hired her to observe Dave.

These days, Sonja is still with WDCS, working as a conservation officer. She lobbies the British Parliament to do more to protect

sea mammals, but she does plenty of fieldwork too. For one thing, she goes on surveys in the Moray Firth, a large body of water off the north coast of Scotland. The Firth is a critical habitat for whales, porpoise, and about 130 of the most northern bottlenose dolphins in the world.

"We want to know if there is anything else, like the minke whales," Sonja explains. "Are there common dolphins around? Are there other dolphins around? Is there anything bigger, like killer whales or humpback whales? They all have been seen in the Firth. But if that's the case that they're resident there, that they're always there, that makes it a really important area."

The inner part of the Moray Firth was designated a Special Area of Conservation in 2005. Still, the WDCS is concerned about the effects of shipping, oil platforms, and wind turbine farms on marine mammals. The tiny population of dolphins is most at risk. "If anything impacts upon them, like too much noise, or there's an oil spill, or the food chain changes or something," she says, "it will impact on these dolphins and they will disappear. Because they don't have anywhere to go, really."

For the surveys on the Firth, Sonja heads out on a rented boat. "A typical day starts about four o'clock in the morning," she says. "We're out when the sun rises. So if it's a good day and it's calm seas, we can do about 12 hours on the boat. It can be really cold standing outside."

During a survey, Sonja and her colleagues take turns at different stations on the boat. Someone watches the water from the bow. Another person is at a computer, logging all the sightings of mammals. And someone else wears a headset, listening to the sounds from the hydrophone, an underwater microphone.

"There's a high frequency component which picks up the harbor porpoise clicks," Sonja explains. "They're too high for us to hear, but we can see them on the computer. Then we have a mid-frequency component, which would pick up whistles of dolphins, for example, and that's what we can hear right away. So we're sitting there listening and watching the screen. There's a program showing what we can't hear, basically."

Sonja loves being outside and seeing dolphins, porpoises, and whales. But it takes lots and lots of patience. "Sometimes it can be really hard work because you're watching blue, blue, blue all day long, and you might not see anything," she

FUNNY NAMES, TRAGIC FATES

If someone called you a two-streaked snake-eyed skink or an Abbott's Booby, you'd probably take it as an insult. But the truth is skinks and boobies are animals with funny names – and very unfunny circumstances. The two-streaked snake-eyed skink is a small reptile found in Armenia, Azerbaijan, and a few other countries. According to the International Union for Conservation of Nature (IUCN), the skink is threatened because of the loss and degradation of its habitat. Abbott's Booby is a large, endangered seabird found only on Christmas Island in the Indian Ocean. The IUCN says destruction of nesting habitat, extreme weather, and super-colonies of yellow crazy ants have put the black-and-white boobies at serious risk. You can learn more about these and hundreds of other endangered animals by visiting the IUCN Red List of Threatened Species website at www.iucnredlist.org.

says. "You start imagining 'Oh, was that a fin? Was that a fin? What was that? And then you realize it might have just been a small wave or something. Your eyes start playing tricks on you. It's just lovely to be outside. If it's a lovely day, there couldn't be any better place to be, really."

As Sonja tries to save dolphins and other sea life, she is winning waves of praise from colleagues in the marine mammal world. "Sonja is extremely dedicated and passionate about her work with cetaceans and marine conservation in general," says Dr. Kevin Robinson, Director of the Cetacean Research and Rescue Unit in Scotland. "What makes her rather exceptional, however, is that she has pursued a somewhat unique career in the field of marine mammal sciences, having worked extensively as a field scientist, academic, and bureaucrat for both government and

non-profit sectors. This has provided her with an eclectic background and experience which I feel gives her an insight and application over and above many of her co-workers and peers."

As she looks to her future, one of Sonja's goals is to share her knowledge. She wants to help people have a better understanding of the amazing creatures of the sea. But no matter where her career takes her, no matter how many whales and dolphins she sees, she will never forget her six weeks watching a girl named Dave.

"I would like to just know she's just roaming free somewhere and she found the way out of her own prison," Sonja says. "But I have this feeling that she might not be alive anymore."

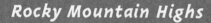

Rocky Mountain Highs

LINDSAY COLLINS, Outdoor Adventure Guide

If the thought of spending your life glued to an office chair in a cubicle the color of stale oatmeal makes you want to scream, picture this as an alternative:

The jagged peaks of the Canadian Rockies jutting into a baby blue sky. Meadows full of flowers. Mountain air so sweet you want to taste it. Clouds close enough to touch. Steamy suppers by a campfire. Horses, not cars. And, occasionally, close encounters with cougars, moose, and cranky grizzly bears.

For the last three summers, that's just what Lindsay Collins experienced when she went to work as a back-country guide in Alberta. "It's majestic and awesome," says the lively 22-year-old community college student and modern-day cowgirl. "You can get up at 6:00 a.m. and go down to the meadow, and you can see a hundred elk walking through the field. Nature is everything there. There are no motorized vehicles allowed. There are no people there. It's just completely cut off from the outside. It's like another world."

❝The happy trails of Alberta are heaven to Lindsay. With its log lodges, stunning scenery, and stables of sleek, even-tempered horses, the ranch is the perfect place to get some work experience – and enjoy a break from the noise and rush of civilization.❞

Lindsay lives on Cape Breton Island on the east coast of Canada. But when summer hits, she heads west to work for a ranch in Alberta's spectacular Kananaskis Valley. (Think Brokeback Mountain. Most of that movie was shot in Alberta.) In her white

cowboy hat, jeans, and well-worn leather boots, she takes groups of tourists on trail rides and pack trips through the Rockies. For the cool-headed, horse-loving Lindsay, having the ultimate eco-adventure job just comes naturally.

"I've always been interested in the outdoors," she says. "I was one of the kids that was out playing in mud puddles and digging in the dirt and things like that, so it was always normal for me to be outside. Mom used to kick me out when I was little and say 'don't come back till the streetlights turn on.' I started riding horses when I was 17 or so. In Cape Breton, I worked in a barn, and I did trail rides all along. And then I decided to go out West."

The happy trails of Alberta are heaven to Lindsay. With its log lodges, stunning scenery, and stables of sleek, even-tempered horses, the ranch is the perfect place to get some work experience — and enjoy a break from the noise and rush of civilization. When she first arrived three years ago, Lindsay started by leading trail rides lasting a day or less. But before long, she knew she wanted to lead pack trips. "That's when you go out for an extended period of time, you live in a tent, and you go on crazy trail rides and stuff," she says. "I finally got to go on one my first year, and they really enjoyed how I worked. So my idea was to say 'if you guys want me to come back and work for you, I'll be half a trail guide and half a pack trip guide.'"

Lindsay got what she wanted. And this summer, she led plenty of pack trips, some with as many as 20 tourists. Each group spent up to a week in the wilderness, pitching tents, sleeping

under the sky, and exploring the wonders of the Rockies. Lindsay says she was so busy she was practically living in the bush, taking only one half-day off every week. It was tough, tiring, utterly amazing work. "I really enjoy how quiet it is," she says. "Just being out in nature, just living off the land. If something breaks or goes wrong, there's nobody there to help you. You have to figure it out on your own."

By now, Lindsay is a master of mountain survival. She can cook up campfire feasts of chicken, spaghetti, and corn on the cob. She chops wood as well as any lumberjack. She sets up solar electric fences to keep animals out of the campsites. And when someone dislocates a thumb or gets a bad cut, she knows just what to do.

"'... we just sat there. The bear charged me. My horse stood. The bear did it again.'"

Sometimes, when things get dangerous, Lindsay's skills and cool head save the day. Like the time she was leading more than a dozen tourists on an "extreme ride" on a perilously narrow mountain trail. The horses were clip-clopping along just a couple of feet from a steep, 1,000-foot (304-meter) drop. (To put it into heart-stopping perspective, that's more than two-thirds as high as the Empire State Building.) Suddenly, something went wrong. "A woman's hat blew off in the wind," Lindsay says. "And a horse in the back got all spooked. The hat scared him, and he spun around. And then the other horses got spooked, and somebody fell off his horse."

As soon as Lindsay saw what was happening, she calmed the animals, made sure the man who had fallen was OK, and, of

course, had him climb right back on that horse. "It was pretty easy," she says. "I sorted it out. You just have to be so level-headed that it's unbelievable."

That level head of Lindsay's comes in handy when she finds herself face to snout with a grizzly bear. One of the burly brown beasts took her by surprise when she was leading a trail ride near the ranch. "The bear actually charged me," she says. "But my horse was good, so I just told everybody 'there's a grizzly bear. Stay calm. Don't make any sudden movements. The horse is enough to scare it away.' So we just sat there. The bear charged me. My horse stood. The bear did it again. And then he walked off into the bushes."

Lindsay's adventure skills and the beauty of the Rockies leave a big impression on visitors, some of whom come from as far away as England and New Zealand. "They pretty much say it's the experience of a lifetime," she says. "I'm still in contact with a whole bunch of them. A bunch have e-mailed me pictures and things like that. They want to keep in touch. They say it's the most amazing thing they've ever done, and they would do it again in a heartbeat."

Co-workers at the ranch are just as impressed with Lindsay. "She has moxie," says Robert Richmond, a chef. "She is intelligent and has a lot of skills that serve her well in dealing with the rigors of horse packing. Those skills, along with her personality and work ethic, combine to make for one heck of a back-country guide. Her schooling in forestry, horse training, and first aid

helps her to deal with the kind of situations that often arise up in the mountains. Being able to use an axe is a definite plus!"

Lindsay is back home in Cape Breton now, studying in the Natural Resources Environmental Technology program at the Nova Scotia Community College. Later, she wants to do a degree in environmental science in British Columbia. Beyond that, she dreams of having her own horse, and maybe even a business.

"I really don't know yet what I want to do for a career," she says. "But I think I'm on the right path to something good."

ADVENTURE 101

How cool is this? In this eco-era, you can actually go to school to learn how to lead outdoor adventures. The *Colorado Outdoor Adventure Guide School* (COAGS), for example, promises to help you master things like horsemanship, hiking, backpacking, fly fishing, orienteering, wilderness survival, and camp cooking. No wonder COAGS calls its courses "education vacation"[5] (www.guideschool.com). Loads of other schools around the world are offering outdoor adventure programs these days. Mount Royal College in Calgary, Alberta, has a four-year program leading to a Bachelor of Applied Ecotourism and Outdoor Leadership[6] (www.mtroyal.ca). Who says you can't go to school and kayak at the same time?

Chapter 7

ORGANICALLY
YOURS

Nature Nirvana

ZOË BRADBURY, Organic Farmer

So what's your idea of a perfect, dreamy, never-to-be-forgotten moment?

Maybe it's a first kiss, the kind that makes you all tingly and weak in the knees. Or ripping the wrapping paper off a brand-new video game system on your birthday. Or scoring the winning goal in the last seconds of a game as your whole school screams and chants your name.

Ah yes, we all have dreams. And each one looks different.

Zoë Bradbury found her heaven on a gorgeous September morning in Oregon not long ago. She was alone in a beautiful field of blooming buckwheat plants. The tiny flowers made a white, lacy haze over lime-green leaves. The air was humming with flies and bees. "It was just one of those moments where my vision was totally manifested," says Zoë. "It was that combination of things like 'Wow, I am really living my dream.' Those are pretty intoxicating moments."

Zoë didn't reach nature nirvana by accident. It took work. Old-fashioned, get-your-hands-dirty, sweat-on-your-brow kind of work. That means getting up at dawn. Grazing Barney and Maude, a team of massive draft horses. Building barns and greenhouses. Planting seeds. Hoeing weeds. Harvesting. Going to market with boxes of fresh asparagus, raspberries, and

candy-stripe Chioggia beets. Enduring aches and pains. Falling into bed, dead tired, after 16-hour days. Trying to figure out how to pay for everything. And doing all of the above ... alone.

Yes, Zoë Bradbury is a farmer. An impassioned, super-educated, unshakably determined organic farmer for the 21st century. Her green, chemical-free acres of bliss are in a river valley in south-western Oregon, not far north of the California border. "It's a great landscape," says Zoë. "It's rolling hills, a lot of livestock, forest, and ocean. It's just a very pretty edge of the continent."

Zoë has been a full-time farmer for less than two years. But her love affair with this land has its roots way back in the early 1970s. Although her parents were big-city types from New York and Chicago, they bought 80 acres and a run-down Oregon farmhouse a few miles from the ocean. A daughter, Abby, came along. And then, a few years later, Zoë was born.

For the Bradbury sisters, childhood was an unusual blend of upscale urban and rubber-boot rural. Their father went into politics, eventually becoming president of the Oregon State Senate. Meeting legislators was as natural as canning plums. "We had an interesting split childhood because we'd go visit my dad and sit on the Senate floor and watch them pass resolutions," Zoë says, "and then we'd go home to the farm and help my mom birth lambs."

When she was 16, the bright, ambitious Zoë left the farm and spent two years at a prestigious Massachusetts college

called Simon's Rock. But wherever she traveled, whatever she learned, her heart was always with the spawning salmon, the sheep, and the blackberries of home, and she knew her career would be in agriculture. So, she went to Stanford University, where she studied ecological anthropology with a focus on sustainable agriculture. By the time she graduated, though, her career vision was all about offices, grant applications, and meetings. Not dirt under her fingernails.

"I shot out of Stanford with a fellowship that took me straight to the Institute for Agriculture and Trade Policy in Minneapolis (IATP)," Zoë says. "And I would say that the trajectory I was on was very much about doing sustainable agriculture advocacy and activism in non-profit organizations. So I went to IATP for three months. Then I went back to the west coast and worked for another non-profit in San Francisco doing sustainable agriculture work."

Zoë was doing well in organizations she respected. City life was fast and exciting. But something, as they say, was missing. "After a string of those experiences, I wasn't happy," she says. "And I couldn't really put my finger on why. I was working for these organizations that had these great mission statements that I totally believed in, but I was miserable. I had a sense that one piece of it was that I didn't want to live in a city anymore. The other piece of it was that I really wanted to be growing food, not just advocating for good food."

> ❝ People wondered about this young woman, dressed in muddy jeans and leather boots, grazing her two huge Belgian horses around the fields. ❞

Zoë went to work for another California-based non-profit organization, the Agriculture and Land-Based Training Association (ALBA). The group provides training, equipment, and other support to people who want to become independent organic farmers. "It was great," she says. "But at the same time, I was working for a farmer and doing farmer's markets in San Francisco, and I loved it. I was finally back in it. … I loved direct marketing, and taking those tomatoes to San Francisco, and having people just fawn over your work and really appreciate the beauty and the flavor and significance of farming the way we farm."

But Oregon was calling. And when Zoë returned to her home state, she signed on to co-manage Sauvie Island Organics, a farm on stunning, lush land not far from Portland. "We did community-supported agriculture and sold to restaurants," she says. "I got an amazing grounding in running a farm. I learned a ton … I did ultimately leave the farm and went to get my master's degree in community change and civic leadership with a food systems focus."

Then, finally, it was time. Time for Zoë to return to the farm where she was born. Time to break ground and start something spectacular all on her own. She moved home. And it felt great.

"It was a little overwhelming because I knew the task at hand," she says. "I had to build an enormous amount of infrastructure to get my farm off the ground, but just the actual physical being here

was wonderful. This has always felt like the center of the universe to me. To return to it was really grounding. I didn't ever look back." The farm started out as an empty hayfield, sketches on graph paper, clipboards, seed catalogues, and many, many ideas. Zoë needed a greenhouse, an irrigation system, and a barn, so she found some power tools and did most of the construction herself. She looked for advice on everything from putting raspberries in the ground to choosing fertilizers. Starting a farm isn't cheap, and Zoë had to resort to putting some of her purchases on a credit card. Making her green dream a reality took a truckload of willpower — and grit. "I would say that first year just feels like climbing an endless mountain," Zoë says. "I did it all single-handedly last year with the occasional panic injection of help from my husband or someone else. But I basically pulled it off alone."

It wasn't long before Zoë's farm turned into a local curiosity. People wondered about this young woman, dressed in muddy jeans and leather boots, grazing her two huge Belgian horses around the fields. The land was turning into a dazzling, multi-colored spectacle, with its perfect rows of strawberries, dahlias, and other crops. "We're pretty much the only produce farm in this  area," she says. "Most people do livestock and cranberries. But as far as growing fruit and veggies, people haven't seen it for 50 or 100 years around here, so there was a ton of curiosity stoppers who would just slow down or stop and come in and talk."

Creating a farm has more drama, pain, and ecstasy than any novel. The physical pain is hard to escape. Exhaustion is almost

a way of life. (Zoë says she sleeps like a rock!) And sometimes, there are little disasters. "A wind storm tore off all of my row cover and tied it around a telephone pole," Zoë says. "And there you are, alone in the storm, trying to get it down and unknot it and put it back on. And times like that, it's definitely trying. You can feel like, 'Oh my God, the world is just against me.' But it's also probably good character development because you know it's totally random and it's not about you."

Sometimes, rain turns into the enemy. On one sleepless night, her stomach in knots, Zoë listened to the rain pounding at the roof. She knew it meant green grass for the horses and sheep, but it also meant the ruination of her strawberries, her best cash crop in the summer. "My strawberries were rupturing in the field, the ripe and semi-ripe berries developing rain lesions as red and raw as open wounds," Zoë wrote in her blog, *Diary of a Young Farmer.* "The mold marches in close on the heels of a rainstorm like that. So on Thursday morning, when there

SHINY HAPPY PEOPLE

Ever wonder which country is the greenest – and happiest – in the world? Well, it turns out there's an organization keeping track of these things. The New Economics Foundation (NEF), which is based in London, created a Happy Planet Index. And in 2009, the lucky country topping the list was … drum roll … Costa Rica! Yes, Costa Ricans say they are satisfied with their lives, they live a long time, and they're light when it comes to carbon footprints.[1] The United Kingdom ranked 74th, Canada was 89th, and the United States came in at 114th. Most of the nations in the top 10 of the Happy Planet Index were, like lucky Costa Rica, in Latin America. Arriba!

www.happyplanetindex.org

was light in the grey sky, Danny and I donned our raingear and crawled through the entire strawberry field, filling Rubbermaid totes with soggy berries. The salvaged harvest totaled over 30 gallons, and none of it would go to market."

For Zoë, that kind of pain pales next to the allure of farming. She loves the work because it's so substantial, so tangible. There's nothing abstract about berries and beets. "As much as I value the non-profit work and all the people who have the grit to do it," she says, "there's nothing as satisfying as looking back at a bed of carrots and having it all weeded and clean. It's sort of an instant gratification a lot of times. But it's also one of the most complex and intriguing puzzles, to really figure out how to farm well and in a way that's holistic and ecological. And it tastes so good. You get to enjoy so many parts of it — and be a part of the environment."

In the middle of her first summer on the land, Zoë had the chance to get a different kind of view of her work. Her friend Joe, a cattle farmer and ex-Air Force pilot, offered to take her up in his little yellow airplane. There, in the air, she looked down on her strawberry patch, the block of head lettuce, the deer fence, and the newly ploughed ground. She could even see Barney and Maude. "To see it all there, real, put a lump in my throat," Zoë remembers. "All at once, from Joe's little plane, it was possible to see how far it's come. There is a farm here now."

And then, as she snapped a picture of her beautiful land, Zoë Bradbury found herself living another of those perfect, dreamy, never-to-be-forgotten moments.

Brewing a Career

TOM GARVEY, Brewer

Tom Garvey admits it. His schoolwork suffered this year. And the reason was beer.

"I've spent most of the semester working on that more than my schoolwork," says the easy-going 22-year-old college student from Oakville, Ontario, Canada. "So I've kind of taken a beating in the marks. But it's been fun."

OK, it's not what you're thinking. Tom Garvey is positively passionate about the sudsy stuff, but he's no party animal. In fact, he's building a career on beer. He dreams of owning a beer company one day. And he's been spending his evenings and weekends apprenticing at a microbrewery, learning the craft of creating bold, bodacious brewskies.

❝❝ Tom Garvey is positively passionate about the sudsy stuff, but he's no party animal. ❞❞

"I've always liked doing stuff with my hands and being able to step back and see the fruits of my labor pretty plainly," Tom says. "I didn't want to get into a job where I was surrounded by people who hated what they were doing. That's one of things that drew me. I can't see myself sitting right next to this guy constantly complaining, or I would become one of those people."

Growing up, Tom thought about becoming an architect or a doctor. But his heart wasn't in it. After high school, he became

an apprentice automotive mechanic, only to realize that fixing cars and trucks wasn't his thing either. "Then I read a magazine article about a man who hated his job in a lab, quit, and became a brewer," Tom says. "I had never considered that an option, so that's why I went back to school."

Tom enrolled in a chemical engineering technology program at Sheridan College. As part of that, he will spend a year studying environmental technology. He says a brewer-to-be probably doesn't really need the environmental part. But when he read about climate change in Tim Flannery's book *The Weather Makers*, Tom felt inspired to learn about green technology. "[The book] sort of shocked me," Tom says. "We have to be more conscious of what we're doing. If I am going to do this, why not take the extra year and learn how to use green energy? Learn what are effective sources of green energy, and apply them."

Tom could be on to something. There's a big green buzz in the beer biz these days. With brewers around the world raising a toast to Mother Earth with new, eco-friendly drinks, green beer isn't just for St. Patrick's Day anymore. A brewery in Colorado, for example, boasts that it lovingly cares for the planet and honors natural resources. The company treats its own wastewater at the plant, uses wind power, and even hosts a bicycle festival. Across the pond, meanwhile, a big brewery is producing what it calls "the United Kingdom's first carbon-neutral beer."

To get ready to make his own splash in the beer industry, Tom is working at a microbrewery just up the street from his home. He's learning everything he can from the brewmaster. "I have voiced to him that someday I'd like to own my own brewery," Tom says. "He's showing me the ins and outs of it, where everything goes, where everything comes from. And that's what I'm doing with the brewery now. Just playing around. Making terrible beer. Making messes."

BREWSKIES AND BIKES

Some jobs come with cool green perks these days. Take the New Belgium Brewing Company in Fort Collins, Colorado. The environmentally friendly brewer gives each employee a free bike after a year on the job. Employees host the Tour de Fat bike race once a year.[2] And the company holds an outdoor "Bike-in Cinema" on the front lawn in the summer.[3]
www.newbelgium.com

The brewery has poured a pint or two of eco-friendliness into its operations. The small team of workers avoids wasting water and electricity, and farmers pick up the "spent" grains (the ones with no more sugars) to use as feed for cows or fertilizer. It's all good for the Earth — and the brewery's bottom line. "In the long run," Tom says, "it's cheaper to do things environmentally than it is to be wasteful.

But Tom and his colleagues are already moving on to greener pastures — literally. They're busy setting up a tiny brewery at a pioneer village popular with tourists in Toronto. They'll brew up a rich, dark ale as visitors watch. And they'll do it old-school. *Really* old-school. Using a fireplace, a barrel, and a copper kettle, they'll make beer the way it was made in

Upper Canada back in the 1860s. "We're putting in almost like a nano-scale brewery," Tom says. "It's going to do maybe 300 liters (79 gallons) a week. Very, very small amounts."

Small amounts, yes. But the little brewery at the village will be a big step in Tom's career. It will also be one of the most environmentally friendly breweries in Canada. Hops are already growing at the pioneer village, and Tom plans to start growing barley there too. His dream is to create a "one-mile beer," with all of the ingredients coming from within one mile of

❝ 'I bet a painter feels the same way, stepping back and seeing the finished canvas," he says. "Except my art is in a cup. That's the best part.' ❞

the brewery. "We're going back to all-natural, organic brewing, with everything sort of kept locally," Tom explains. "And with no fuel costs, no transport, nothing like that. I've actually been looking at a donkey in a donkey sanctuary that I want to get to carry the water for the brewery. So that's about the coolest thing that I have done."

The even cooler thing is that the little green brewery idea could wind up flowering like hops. Another pioneer village has already been in touch with Tom and the rest of the team to ask about setting up a mini-brewery of its own. "I am hoping that once [the first brewery] gets up and started and we get the barley field going, it'll sort of be self-sustaining, and not really require too much work on my part," Tom says. "I'm pretty excited. I think it would be awesome if every pioneer village had a little brewery."

As Tom immerses himself in the beer industry, he's more and more convinced that green beer is the future. To him, brewing in an eco-friendly way is more important than ever. Consumers, he says, are looking for it. "You sort of have to be cutting-edge here," he says. "People are so tired of preservatives and all these GMOs (genetically-modified organisms). I think it's going to be even more important to have an all-organic beer or product.

Any way that you can cut down on the changes that you're making to these Earth products, the better it's going to be."

Tom's budding brewing skills are getting attention from his friends. A few have come by the microbrewery to check out the malting, the mashing, and the great big kegs. "When they hear I work at a brewery, a lot of the guys want to sit down and chat," Tom says. "All the girls seem to, like, flock away. I don't think women are very interested in beer."

Personal popularity (or the lack thereof!) aside, Tom is happy in his work. He doesn't have to sit in an office, each day is different, he gets to create something that people will enjoy, and he's even being kind to Mother Earth. "I bet a painter feels the same way, stepping back and seeing the finished canvas," he says. "Except my art is in a cup. That's the best part."

Cheers, Tom.

A Budding Career

Java Joy

JULIA CLARK, *Program Associate, Scientific Certification Systems (SCS)*

AGE: 26

ECO-CAREER: Julia is a program associate with California-based Scientific Certification Systems, which does independent (or "third-party") certification of companies' claims of sustainability, food quality, and food purity.

GREENSPIRATIONS: Julia grew up in British Columbia, Canada. Her father is a naturalist who works for the B.C. Ministry of Environment. "My whole childhood was just filled with camping and nature walks that would always take a really long time because he would be pointing out what all the plants were. He has a very deep way of looking at the Earth, and I think that that always rubbed off on me."

VILLAGE VOICES: In her teens, Julia traveled to Ottawa, Denmark, France, Honduras, and other countries to take part in Children's International Summer Villages (CISV). The camps bring together kids and teens from all over the world. "I think that that's where I started seeing the relationship between social issues and environmental issues, which is really what my work is centered around now."

ECO-ED 101: Julia is a graduate of the prestigious Lester B. Pearson United World College of the Pacific in British Columbia, as well as the ecology-drenched College of the Atlantic (COA) in Maine.

JAVA JOB: At Scientific Certification Systems, Julia works in the "responsible sourcing" division. Her main task is to work with Starbucks on its commitment to social and environmental responsibility. Starbucks coffee comes from farms in Central America, South America, Indonesia, East Africa,

and other parts of the world. Julia helps organizations in those countries learn how to inspect the farms and report back to SCS. "Essentially, the program ensures that workers are being treated fairly, that they're meeting minimum wage standards, that there's no discrimination or child labor going on," she says. "The program seeks to encourage, wherever possible, reductions in the use of pesticides."

COFFEE PERKS: "I really enjoy working in the green business movement. This job is providing me with an incredible amount of skill building, and learning, and language building, and travel, and everything that I could want out of a job right now."

THE GREEN ECONOMY: "Most of my friends work in green businesses, and they're thriving. It's really incredible to see the companies that are doing well are these green businesses that are in this niche market. They're strong, and they're going to be incredibly well-poised to explode."

ECO-ADVICE: "I think the most important thing is just to keep your eyes and ears and mind open to opportunities that cross your way – because there are so many incredible things going on in the world right now."

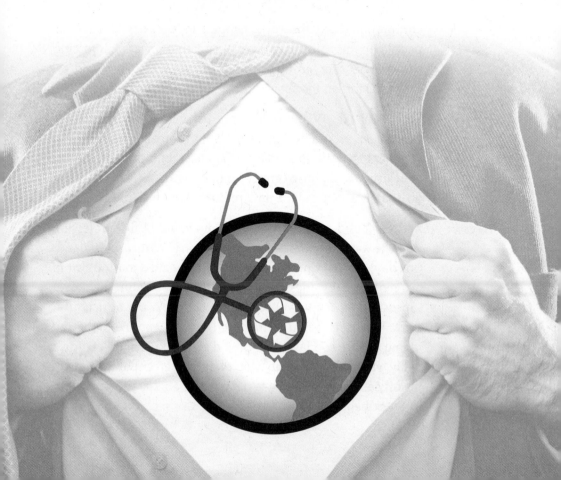

Chapter 8

ECO
HEALTH

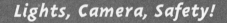

Lights, Camera, Safety!

ANDREW WALSH, Environmental Health Practitioner

When Andrew Walsh decided to become an environmental health practitioner, he had no idea his career choice would lead to close encounters with water buffalo, an Indonesian tribe, and Kylie Minogue.

For the last two years, the 27-year-old Londoner has been working as a safety advisor for the British Broadcasting Corporation (BBC), the world's largest broadcaster. While many people in his profession are inspecting meats, enforcing smoking bans, or hunting down rats and cockroaches, Andrew is riding high on the show-biz side of environmental health.

"The BBC makes TV and radio, of course, but we're there to help them make programs," he says. "So it's a really enabling job. Whether they want to send a team to the Arctic, or to the desert, or to just go and film in central London, we are there to help them do it safely and to get the right resources and the right controls."

Andrew found out about the environmental health profession when he was a teen in the town of Preston in northwest England. One day, an environmental health officer paid a routine visit to his mother's business. (She was involved with the Royal Lancashire Agricultural Society, which runs a big agricultural show.) Far from being intimidated, young Andrew found the roving enviro-cop fascinating. "I'd always known that I didn't really want a career or job which was 100 percent of the time in the office," he says. "I like to get out and about, and not just to be stuck behind a desk."

Sensing a flicker of ambition, Andrew's mother arranged for him to spend two weeks shadowing environmental health officers from a small local authority. "I went into businesses and saw the good, the bad, and the ugly of environmental health," says Andrew, who watched the officers grapple with everything from filthy food establishments to noise complaints. "Just a very quick snapshot. But that was enough, really, to make me think, 'Ah, this is something that I'd quite like to know more about.'"

So, after high school graduation, Andrew enrolled in a four-year environmental health program at Manchester Metropolitan University. He says he was drawn to environmental health partly because of its diversity. "I thought, 'this is a job where I can never get bored,'" he says. "Whether it be food safety, or health and safety, or environmental protection, or even meat inspection or pollution, there's just so much there to choose from. It's almost like lots of professions in one."

Once Andrew had his degree, it was a cinch finding a good job. He went to work doing health and safety enforcement for a municipality, eventually becoming a public health coordinator. Around that time, England was counting down to July 1, 2007, the day virtually all enclosed public spaces and workplaces in the country went smoke-free. "It took quite a lot for that change to happen in the authority that I was in," Andrews says. "It had higher smoking prevalence rates than other areas. The hospitality industry was quite against it."

Once the ban was in place, Andrew helped enforce it. He had the power to fine or prosecute people who broke the law. But he usually let them off with a stern warning. "One evening, we walked into one particular pub, and there were two guys smoking at the bar, and the landlord was smoking as well," Andrew recalls. "So I just took him aside and said, 'Where have you been for the last six months? Do you not know that the law has come in?' He was quite apologetic."

Later that year, Andrew noticed an ad for a safety advisor position with the BBC. He liked the idea of moving to London and working for a massive company. So he applied, went for an interview, and got the job. Before long, Andrew was lending his enviro expertise to wildly popular TV shows like *Crime Watch*, *Last Man Standing*, and a soap opera called *EastEnders*. "Whatever they want to do," he says, "we throw a safety angle on it."

Just as he was getting used to being around Big Ben and Buckingham Palace, Andrew found himself in a remote section of forest on the Indonesian island of Sumbawa. As part of the *Last Man Standing* series, six super-athletes were going to compete against a tribe in the local sport of water buffalo racing. "Some [members of the tribe] had never seen a white person before in the flesh, so that was interesting," he says. "With the filming, we tend to go to places that you would never get to visit in normal life, just as a tourist or whatever. ... You've got to be very sensitive, really, to the fact that you're in a completely different country. You want to bring a TV crew there

and just shine the light on what they do. We're always really well-received. And you meet some brilliant people."

Before the *Last Man Standing* cameras could start rolling, Andrew had to make sure that no one was going to get hurt in the heart-pounding race. As part of the preparations, he decided to try buffalo racing himself. "Basically there's two buffalo, and you're on this tiny little peak of wood in the middle of them," he says. "And they charge across a paddy field. And you've basically got to ride it like a jockey. The aim is to get across to the other side and then guide the buffalo over this magic stick that the shaman has willed you to go over. So it's almost like a target race."

THE TOP GREEN JOBS

Wondering where the green work is? ECO Canada, the country's leading authority on environmental jobs, put together this list of the hottest green careers in Canada:

1. Environmental Engineer
2. Environmental Technologist/Technician
3. Conservation Biologist
4. Green Information System (GIS) Analyst
5. Environmental Communications Officer [1]

Andrew made sure the athletes were well-trained and knew how to interact with the buffalo. The animals weighed more than a ton each, and there was a risk of being kicked. "Then, of course, there's: how do you film it safely?" he explains. "Where do you put the cameras in such a position that they're not going to get hit by this charging buffalo?"

But Andrew does more than make sure the people on camera are safe. When a BBC show is shooting on location, he also has to think about environmental issues. "What are [the TV

crewmembers] doing there?" he says. "Could they contaminate the ground? Are they burning anything? Sometimes we do fire or pyrotechnic effects. You've got to think about the environmental side there. You're quite multidisciplinary, so you can think in different ways about all the different risks. Not just how someone might get harmed, but how the environment can as well. So that again is quite interesting."

In the end, millions of Brits watched the Indonesian buffalo race on TV. But even success in Sumbawa wasn't the pinnacle

of Andrew Walsh's career. His favorite moment happened back in London, on the night of the BBC's huge *Children In Need* charity telethon. In the past, superstars like the Spice Girls, Kylie Minogue, and Annie Lennox had performed at the annual extravaganza, which raises millions of dollars for disadvantaged children across the United Kingdom. Seeing an opportunity, Andrew offered to work as a runner for the show.

"I was walking down a corridor," he says, "and Kylie [Minogue] and her entourage walked down at the same time towards me. And I stepped aside, and she gave me a little smile. So I thought that was a nice moment."

Andrew's parents describe him as a "likeable lad," and they say they're proud of his achievements. "Who would have thought that his interest in environmental health would have been nurtured by two weeks of work experience at a local

council environmental health department while still at school?" says Philip Walsh, Andrew's father. "He definitely knew it was for him. He has succeeded through sheer hard work, enthusiasm, and his determination to improve himself."

Andrew is one of many people who have environmental careers without being environmental activists. He says he's green at the consumer level, and he likes to play his part in recycling. But what he really loves is the business side of environmental health. "The regulation, the food safety, the health-and-safety kind of side," he says. "When you're actually dealing with businesses, as opposed to the pure environment side."

And diversity, the thing that attracted him to the profession in the first place, is still the thing he enjoys the most. "One minute, I'll be working with a production that is going reindeer herding in Siberia," he says, "and helping them think about evacuation plans and having the right medic support. Or the next, dealing with a consumer program ... doing covert filming."

For Andrew, the other thrills of working for the world's biggest broadcaster are being around creative people, trying new things, and pushing boundaries. "My job is to just think solely about the risk," he says. "Anything is possible. It's just you've got to have a little bit of time. ...You have to make TV, and you don't want to completely put it in cotton wool. You've just got to control the risks."

After all, at the end of Andrew Walsh's day, the show must go on.

Revealing Beauty's Ugly Side

NNEKA LEIBA, Environmental Health Researcher

If Oprah's people call you a role model, you know you're doing something right.

That's just what happened to Nneka Leiba. The 29-year-old is with the Environmental Working Group (EWG), an American non-profit organization on a mission to protect public health and the environment. *O, The Oprah Magazine* featured Nneka, along with EWG founder Ken Cook, in an article called "The New Eco Role Models."

> **❝ But EWG is warning people to think twice before slathering on the lotions, pouring the bubbles into baby's bath, or breaking out the bucks for the latest anti-aging creams. ❞**

Growing up in Jamaica in the 1990s, Nneka never dreamed she'd get a nod from one of the world's greenest, richest, most powerful celebrities. So when the magazine story came out, it splashed up a sea of excitement.

"It was fabulous, it was fabulous," says Nneka. "I started getting calls from people back home who saw it, and that was amazing. … I have one copy and my mom has one copy, and I think all of my friends have a copy. I think we really boosted the sales of *O* magazine."

Nneka, a green whirlwind with three environment-related university degrees, is one of the people behind the ragingly popular "Skin Deep." That's EWG's online safety database for cosmetics and personal care products. If you're wondering what's in your lipsticks, deodorants, or anything else that

touches your skin, you can run searches on the "Skin Deep" website. With one click, you'll find out whether your product could be hazardous to your health. If the website's database of 42,000 products doesn't include your bubble bath, balm, or blush, you can type in the ingredients and get an instant toxicity report. You could say "Skin Deep" reveals the ugly side of beauty.

"I, like most people, was completely unaware of the lack of regulations in cosmetics," Nneka says. "It's just really enlightening to look at the database and look at the actual chemicals that you're being exposed to on a daily basis. And you put on these personal care products once or twice a day, every single day, and nobody is looking over it. It's just astounding."

A lot of people think skin-care products must be safe if they're in the stores. But EWG is warning people to think twice before slathering on the lotions, pouring the bubbles into baby's bath, or breaking out the bucks for the latest anti-aging creams. They say lax laws in the United States are

RUBBING IT IN

The Environmental Working Group (EWG) isn't the only organization fighting to plump up the safety level of your powders and perfumes, aftershaves and antiperspirants. EWG has teamed up with Friends of the Earth, the National Black Environmental Justice Network, the Breast Cancer Fund, and several other groups to create the Campaign For Safe Cosmetics. The Campaign pushes skin-care product manufacturers to stop using chemicals linked to cancer, birth defects, and other health problems.[2] There have been some victories. For one, about 1,000 companies have signed the Compact For Safe Cosmetics, a pledge to make products safer.[3]

allowing the multi-billion-dollar cosmetics industry to use hazardous chemicals in skin-care products. "There are not enough, if any at all, regulations for cosmetics," says Nneka. "It's just horrible."

A lot of Americans, apparently, are listening. There have been more than 107-million product searches on the website since "Skin Deep" started in 2004. Products are rated on a scale of one to 10. A score of zero to two suggests a product is pretty safe, while three to six points mean a moderate hazard. Products scoring between seven and 10 — those are the ones in the red zone — are considered highly hazardous. (One popular moisturizer, for example, rates a nine for ingredients connected to cancer, developmental toxicity, allergies, and other problems.) It's information more and more consumers are craving. "Every single time we go anywhere and mention 'Skin Deep,'" Nneka says, "there is somebody that has said, 'Oh my God, I love that site.'"

Nneka works at EWG's headquarters in Washington, D.C. But she grew up in Jamaica's capital city, Kingston. The island nation is a tropical, turquoise-water paradise pulsating with reggae and saturated in sunshine. As a child, Nneka spent time in Jamaica's rural areas, enjoying the rivers and gorgeous greenery. "When you grow up in such a beautiful place," she says, "you just don't even realize how great the environment is and how much it needs to be protected."

As a teenager, Nneka became more aware of some of Jamaica's environmental problems. Precious beach sand was being mined

for use in construction. Bauxite mining, hugely important to the island's economy, was causing environmental damage. Some Jamaicans, meanwhile, were reckless with their trash. "People thought that as long as you threw things out into the sea it would dilute it enough, and it wouldn't have an effect," Nneka says. "But we all know that that's not true. A lot of it has to do with poor income areas, where recycling, for example, is just not the priority. So that was a big issue."

Nneka's life changed one day when she was about 17 years old. An environmentalist came to speak to her high school class. Listening to the presentation, Nneka was on fire with inspiration. "I was always in the environmental club, so I always had this love," she says. "But then to realize that you could make it into something more, I think, really touched a nerve."

Nneka decided to go to college and take environmental studies. There was just one problem: The Jamaican university she was going to attend didn't have such a program. "About five of us wanted to do an environmental program," Nneka says. "So they made one, and the five of us were the pilot class."

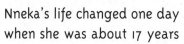

TEEN POWER

Young people from across the United States are banding together to demand changes in the cosmetics industry. Teens For Safe Cosmetics is a California-based coalition that informs teens about "an all-encompassing eco-lifestyle, beginning with greener choices in cosmetics and personal care products." One of the group's big projects is Lips Against Lead, a national campaign to ban lead in lipstick.[4] You can read more at www.teensturninggreen.org.

Nneka earned a bachelor's degree in environmental biology and a master's in zoology in her home country. Still thirsty for knowledge, she decided to take her career in the environmental health direction. She moved to the United States and did a master's degree in public health at the Johns Hopkins University.

> **One of the hardest things in environmental health is talking about stuff that people don't see a connection with immediately.**

"After that, I started applying for jobs and looking around. And Environmental Working Group, which is where I am now, just seemed to really encompass all that I wanted to do."

For Nneka, being featured in *O* magazine is just one of the satisfying things about working for "Skin Deep." "I enjoy seeing things like the 107-million searches," Nneka says. "I like when we work really hard on something and it makes a connection. One of the hardest things in environmental health is talking about stuff that people don't see a connection with immediately. So if something is toxic or has a hazard, it doesn't mean that it's going to burn you immediately. It's really hard trying to convince somebody that in 20 years, this could happen. So when you start to see some sort of recognition and some grassroots movements, people get really involved."

Nneka helps people understand not only what's in their skin care products, but what's lurking in their drinking water too. EWG spent more than two years investigating tap water from across the United States. It found a total of 260 contaminants (including pesticides, ammonia, and arsenic) in tap water from 42 states. EWG now has an online National Tap Water Quality Database, which is like a water version of "Skin Deep."

"We contact all of the states, and the state agencies send us their water quality testing information, and we put that online," Nneka explains. "So you can click on your state and find out how many contaminants were found in your water."

Still, EWG doesn't want you to rush out and buy a truckload of bottled water. Quite the opposite, really. Nneka and a few of her colleagues wrote a report about the quality — or lack thereof — of bottled water. "Our tests strongly indicate that the purity of bottled water cannot be trusted," the report says, suggesting that ads with dreamy images of mountain springs lead consumers to believe bottled water is far better than tap water. According to EWG's study, some bottled water from major chain stores was "chemically indistinguishable" from tap water. The only striking difference, says the report, is the price tag.[8]

BUMMER

Some green warriors are even tackling diapers. Each day, millions and millions of disposable diapers head to landfills around the world, and they can take hundreds of years to decompose.[5] (Ewww!) A company in England is trying to give that the bum's rush. Knowaste has found a way to recycle disposable "nappies." The company will wash and mechanically separate diapers. The plastics will be sold and made into bicycle helmets, roof tiles, and other products. Methane gas from the "muck" in the diapers will be converted into green energy.[6] Knowaste says for every ton of diaper waste that's recycled, 882 pounds (400 kilograms) of wood, 5,120 cubic feet (145 cubic meters) of natural gas, and 307,237 cubic feet (8,700 cubic meters) of water is saved.[7] And baby, that's good news.

"We started promoting reusable stainless steel bottles," Nneka says. "And so many people are walking around with stainless

steel bottles now and not drinking bottled water. That's a huge plus, because everybody was drinking bottled water a couple of years ago. We don't ever take full credit for anything, but even just slight connections with a change in the population's behavior is a huge deal."

Nneka says she wants to keep working in the non-profit world, and she may go back to university and earn a doctorate one day. Whatever happens, she's devoted to helping people lead healthier, greener lives. "It's not the best gross-salary type job," she says. "But if you're really passionate about something, the joys that it gives you to see successes are so worth it that you should just really stick to it."

Now those are the words of a role model. Take it from Oprah.

The Green Doctor is In

SARAH LESPERANCE, Physician

As we all know, seventh grade isn't easy. And I'm not talking about just the history and the algebra. Seventh-graders have to deal with everything from body image issues to bullying.

But what if, on top of all the usual pains of adolescence, you had to cope with a crisis in the family? What if you found out one of your parents had cancer?

Sarah Lesperance has been there. When she was in seventh grade, her mother was diagnosed with breast cancer. And

through her teen years, Sarah had to learn to live with that sad, inescapable reality.

"It was pretty difficult as a teenager, especially in high school," says Sarah, who's now 26 years old. "Not many other people were having to deal with such a big life event ... and I had some friends that were afraid to say too much, or didn't know what to say, and things like that. But I had some good friends that helped me through it."

> **" ... sometimes, inspiration can trickle from tragedy. Partly because of what her mother went through, Sarah has just become *Dr.* Sarah Lesperance. "**

Sarah's mother, a nuclear physicist, spent years trying to figure out what had caused the cancer. She cut back on meat, started buying more organic foods, had the tap water tested, and even had radiation from the TV measured. "She looked at everything in our environment for causes for this," Sarah says. "So that was probably a big thing that stuck with me."

When Sarah was 17, her mother passed away. But sometimes, inspiration can trickle from tragedy. Partly because of what her mother went through, Sarah has just become *Dr.* Sarah Lesperance.

"I don't know if it's quite sunk in today, since it has been sort of a long haul the last month in terms of studying," says Sarah, taking time to chat the morning after her very last day of medical school at the University of Ottawa. "It's definitely an exciting point because the four years of medical school are pretty grueling at certain points. You study hard, you don't get much sleep, you work long hours."

❝More and more medical students and doctors are finding ways of blending their careers with their environmental passions.❞

Finishing medical school is, of course, a monumental accomplishment all on its own. But Sarah isn't only an M.D. She's an environmental activist who somehow finds space in her busy life for fighting ecological ills like pesticides. "I don't know how many times I sent messages or called and mobilized big groups of my classmates to get involved, to sign petitions," she says. "We had one petition we sent off to the government that had about 300 signatures."

Sarah may be part of a trend in medicine. More and more medical students and doctors are finding ways of blending their careers with their environmental passions. "Medicine is changing," Sarah says. "The people that come into medical school now are from incredibly diverse backgrounds, and medicine is really a career that you can make what you want it to be. You have a lot of flexibility. ... You have a very powerful voice to make your concerns heard about what's happening in the environment."

Sarah found that voice partly because of a life-changing trip to Guatemala a few years ago. She met community leaders and learned about the genocide of Mayan people in that Central American country in the 1980s. "There was one community we went to where a mass grave had been exhumed," Sarah recalls. "The bodies were being returned to the community members. They were all laid out in a church, and family members were going around trying to identify their loved ones, just by the shreds of clothes. ... They really wanted us there, the

Guatemalans. They wanted us to take pictures. They wanted all of this brought back and shared with people. And it was a really powerful experience there. But also to learn the power that we have as people in the more developed world. We can go back to our governments and say 'Hey, this is what's happening here.'"

The trip inspired Sarah to start thinking about medical school. She wanted the skills and knowledge to be able to advocate for better health. But with her strong social and environmental conscience, she wondered where she would fit in the medical milieu.

Then, not long after starting medical school, she was on a train between Toronto and Ottawa. As if by destiny, she sat next to the president of the Canadian Association of Physicians for the Environment (CAPE). He told her medical school didn't have to change her values, ideas, and other things that were important to her. "He gave me this little pep talk in terms of 'hang in there, and you can make it what you want it to be,'" Sarah says. "Then he gave me his business card and said, 'Well, we're looking for some students to help us out with CAPE projects, and give me a shout if you want to get involved.' And that's how it started. It was a pretty neat chance meeting."

Sarah kept the business card and made the call. Before long, she was in the middle of several CAPE campaigns to fight pesticide use in Canadian communities. She wrote anti-pesticide opinion pieces for newspapers. She met with politicians. And she encouraged other med students to write

letters and support the campaigns. Through it all, she began to see that doctors-in-training have credibility and clout. "The idea that physicians have this extra authority or voice," she says, "is something that you can really use for positive change."

People in power must have listened. Just as Sarah was finishing medical school, the province of Ontario brought in a ban on

cosmetic pesticides. The government said using pesticides to control weeds and insects purely for a prettier lawn posed an unnecessary risk to families and pets. "It's definitely something that I'm proud of being a part of," Sarah says. "Once you've got it at the provincial level, that's a pretty strong message."

Sarah's determination to juggle med school and activism has impressed plenty of people, including the top tier at the Canadian Association of Physicians for the Environment. "She was very idealistic," says Gideon Forman, the organization's executive director. "The thing about medical students, they're incredibly busy. They're just weighed down with their course work. And yet she always made time to do this environmental advocacy work. ... I was just really impressed with her willingness to take this on at a time when many students are just so immersed in their studies they can't think of anything else."

Sarah's passion for the planet is painted all over her lifestyle. She bikes a lot, eats organic foods, recycles, and uses the "Skin Deep" website to research ingredients in skin-care products. (See the "Skin Deep" story in the profile of Nneka Leiba earlier

in this chapter.) You could even say Sarah is married to the cause. At her wedding a couple of years ago, she wore a hand-sewn gown made of hemp silk and served local wines and delicacies. She and her husband even bought rings made of recycled platinum.

Now, with medical school behind her, Sarah is packing up and getting ready to move to Moncton on Canada's east coast. After a two-year residency at local hospitals, she will be ready to start her career as a family physician. She says standing up for environmental causes will continue to be a part of her life. "I'm sure it's going to have some sort of a role," she says. "Probably a big part will be the advocating for changes in whatever community I'm living in, looking around at those environmental factors and trying to make some changes there."

But before she leaves Ottawa, there's something Sarah has to pick up: a medical diploma. Her father and other family will be there to cheer her on. And as she graduates, she will be remembering the person who helped inspire her medical career. "(My mother) is not here for this," Sarah says. "But I'm sure she would have been really proud of me too."

No doubt.

Chapter 9

OCEANS
APART

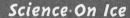

Science·On Ice

ALEXANDRA JAHN, Meteorologist

As a little girl growing up in a duplex on the outskirts of Berlin, Germany, Alexandra Jahn never imagined herself cruising into a cold kingdom of ice, polar bears, and perfect pink sunsets.

But last year, the 29-year-old scientist was on the Arctic Ocean aboard a Canadian Coast Guard research ship. In the eerie still of a September day, her ears covered by the flaps of her blue wool hat, she stared in awe. The icebergs, some of them as big as buildings, were silent white monsters in the mist.

"They were amazing," says Alex, as she likes to be called. "We went over to the Greenland coast, so there were lots of really, really big icebergs. I think they were half as long as the ship. ... We couldn't get too close. If the iceberg flips, and we're under it, then that's it."

Alex was born, appropriately enough, during a very cold February. She was a kid who loved math, physics and geography — and weather patterns fascinated her. "When Alexandra was 12, we made a two-week-long trip on our bikes," recalls her mother, Sonja. "We had many rainy days, and Alexandra began to observe the clouds. She was always warning us of approaching rain and thunderstorms. Her interest in the weather was born."

Alex later did a degree in meteorology at the Free University of Berlin. During her time there, she had a job as a weather observer, peering at the sky through the windows of a tower, classifying clouds, and making radar reports. She thought about becoming a weather forecaster, but she wanted something less routine. So, she decided to move to the cold climes of Montreal, Canada, to do a doctorate in atmospheric and oceanic sciences at McGill University.

In her research, Alex looks at how fresh water from rivers moves through the salty Arctic Ocean. "This is important for many reasons," she says. "First of all, the fresh water from the rivers has an effect on the stability of the surface waters in the Arctic Ocean, and that has important implications for the biological activity in the ocean. … It's also important because river water carries many pollutants, and we need to understand where they end up in order to protect the Arctic."

"The sleek red-and-white floating lab would be Alex's home for one unforgettable month. "

To study the movement of river water in the Arctic, Alex runs computer-simulated climate models. They give her a picture of what's going on in the ocean and the atmosphere. Last September, she was offered the chance to take a break from simulations of the Arctic Ocean and check out the real thing. She packed her warmest clothes, left the chic metropolis of Montreal and flew up to tiny Resolute Bay. High above the Arctic Circle, the village of 200 people is one of the coldest, most northern communities on Earth.

It was an exciting time in Resolute. The CCGS Amundsen, a state-of-the-art icebreaker owned by the Canadian Coast Guard, was visiting. The ship had been at sea for more than a year, making history with an incredible 36,039-mile (58,000-kilometer) research expedition in the Arctic Ocean. The sleek red-and-white floating lab would be Alex's home for one unforgettable month. "There were 40 scientists and 40 crewmembers on the ship," she says. "You had a bunk bed and a desk and closet, and that was it. We had a lot of work to do."

MEGA MARINE MAKEOVER

The CCGS Amundsen icebreaker has a case of multiple identities. The ship was christened The Sir John Franklin back in the 1970s to honor the famous Arctic explorer. Almost 30 years later, it went through a huge, multi-million-dollar retrofit in preparation for its scientific mission in the Arctic Ocean. Along with a new life, the ship got a new name. It was christened CCGS Amundsen in honor of another Arctic explorer, Roald Amundsen.[1] To see amazing pictures of the icebreaker and learn more about Arctic research, check out www.amundsen.ulaval.ca.

The Arctic is a wondrous world of its own, with glassy silver waters, mountains that look like they've been sprinkled with icing sugar and skies right out of a dream. "In the beginning, it was very cloudy," Alex says. "But for the second part of the four weeks, we had very nice weather. It was very sunny. Quite windy though. The ship was moving quite a bit, and a lot of people got seasick. But the sky was often really blue, and we had amazing sunsets."

During her time at sea, Alex used a CTD/Rosette, a round metal cage that holds 24 bottles. The instrument allowed her to collect

> " ... life on a science ship in the Arctic isn't cushy like a Caribbean cruise. "

and test water samples from the cold, dark depths of the Arctic Ocean. "You lower it into the ocean, 32.8 feet (10 meters) from the bottom," she explains. On the way up, you stop it at different depths, and you can close the bottles remotely from the ship."

One thing Alex measured was the salinity — or salt content — of the water. "From the salinity profiles we took, we can infer many things," she explains. "For example, how stable the water column is, as well as if it contains a lot of river water. Salinity measurements give me a picture of where fresh water is present."

As Alex learned, life on a science ship in the Arctic isn't cushy like a Caribbean cruise. Strong winds can make the instruments smash against the side of the ship, so she sometimes couldn't do her work. Besides that, using the ship's satellite phone cost about a dollar a minute, so she didn't call home. And with 40 scientists sharing two computers and one shaky Internet connection, she had to wait in line to send e-mails.

Still, Sonja Jahn was happy about her daughter's Arctic adventure. "One of Alexandra's

HOT AND STEAMY ICELAND

Get shivers when you think about Iceland? Don't. The truth is the country has a lot of hot stuff. The geothermal kind, I mean. Iceland is a highly volcanic island, and that means a huge amount of heat is stored in the earth. That heat is used to produce all the environmentally friendly electricity the locals could ever want.[2] The power is so cheap some sidewalks in Iceland are heated. Watch where you're stepping, Frosty!

career aspirations was to be a captain on the sea," she says. "I think that this dream is still in her mind, and that's why she loves staying on a ship. Polar research is also very fitting for her because she always liked the winter more than the summer."

The trip aboard the Amundsen was huge for Alex's career. For one thing, she says, it was her first chance to do field research. It also gave her a unique opportunity to meet dozens of other young scientists who shared her fascination with the Arctic. "That was very, very inspiring," she says. "That was probably the biggest profit I made from the whole trip. Seeing the Arctic was great, but talking to all these people and finding out about the different kinds of research they do in the Arctic, that was really amazing."

When Alex graduates from McGill, she will be "Dr. Jahn." (Her dad in Germany can't wait to tell people his daughter has a PhD.) She wants to stay in Arctic research, whether it's back home in Europe or someplace else. But whatever happens in her life and career, Alex will never forget the icebergs, the sunsets, and the cold, cold waves of the Arctic Ocean.

"The beauty of the Arctic will always stay in my memory," she says, "and motivate me to do my part to try and conserve it as best I can."

One Highflyer

NICOLE CABANA, Pilot

As one of the worst November hurricanes in history started a lethal rampage across the islands of the Caribbean, Nicole Cabana boarded a jet in Tampa, Florida, and buckled herself into an orange seat.

She wasn't heading north to get away from the wicked weather. Instead, she was about to begin the ultimate flight into danger — and one of the most spectacular adventures of her life. When the nose of the plane lifted off the tarmac, Nicole knew she was heading straight for the eye of the hurricane.

"My family was pretty apprehensive when I told them I was doing it," says the intrepid Nicole, a 30-year-old pilot with the National Oceanic and Atmospheric Administration (NOAA), a federal agency focused on the conditions of the oceans and atmosphere. "It's super important to fly into hurricanes. We do it, and the Air Force does it. With the NOAA planes, we're doing research on the storm."

Nicole, known as Lieutenant Cabana on the job, isn't one of NOAA's official "hurricane hunters," the pilots who fly into storms to collect vitally important data. She usually flies a Twin Otter airplane to survey right whales, harbor seals, and other sea mammals. But every time a hurricane threatens to hit the United States, NOAA sends a specially-equipped plane to measure things such as wind speed, temperature, and pressure. When Nicole heard a Category Four hurricane was blustering its way toward Cuba, she asked to tag along on the mind-blowing, adrenaline-

pumping flight. In the end, the jet flew through the eye of Hurricane Paloma not once, but five times.

As Nicole watched through her window, the plane cut through raging winds, hail, and huge towers of cloud. The sea below was white with foam and monster waves. At one point, she says, the plane hit a powerful downdraft and dropped more than 1,500 feet (457 meters) in less than a minute. "But one thing that I didn't know was that in the exact eye, dead in the center of the storm, the winds are dead calm," Nicole says. "If we were flying around in circles in the center of the eye and we approached too close to the edge of the eye, we would start feeling a lot of turbulence."

Although she's barely out of her 20s, Nicole is already nine years into an amazing, high-flying career with NOAA, the smallest uniformed service in the United States. The job has seen her swim with sharks near Belize, save seals from fishing gear in Hawaii, attend high-level meetings on Capitol Hill, and narrowly escape disaster aboard a small plane in a remote corner of Alaska.

> **Nicole's career is packed with peril – and perks. She has a title and a bright blue uniform, but she didn't have to go to boot camp, she doesn't carry a gun, and she will never have to go to war. She gets to see the world from land, sea, and air. And she will be able to retire when she's in her early 40s.**

Nicole's career is packed with peril — and perks. She has a title and a bright blue uniform, but she didn't have to go to boot camp, she doesn't carry a gun, and she will never have to go to war. She gets to see the world from land, sea, and air. And she will be able to retire when she's in her early 40s.

But one of the greatest parts of the job was being paid to become a pilot. "Flight training, I think, will end up being one of the highlights of my career," says Nicole, who went to flight school in Florida for seven months when she was in her early 20s. "My whole job was to learn how to fly a plane. I didn't have any other office duties. I lived in this great house that was right on the beach. It was really just kind of a carefree and wonderful time in my career."

Nicole always had a passion for the ocean. "I think it's because going to the beach when I was younger was such a special thing," says Nicole, who kick-started her career by doing volunteer work with penguins at an aquarium when she was a teen. "I always had really positive feelings whenever I was near the water. Then when my family moved to Massachusetts, we were right on the water. The ocean is where I go when I need answers or need to feel something larger than myself."

After high school graduation, Nicole moved to the coast of Maine and studied at the College of the Atlantic, where the environment seeps into every aspect of academics and campus life. When she finished her degree, a family friend urged her to check out the opportunities at NOAA, so she spoke with a recruiter. "I was like, well, aside from the whole uniform thing, this sounds like a pretty cool job," she remembers.

Nicole's first assignment was to spend two years at sea aboard McArthur, a 1000-ton scientific research ship. It was an around-the-world

adventure, with voyages to the Gulf of Mexico, the Caribbean, South America, and Hawaii. Nicole navigated and maneuvered the vessel, and she helped launch small submarines.

"That's really high-stakes stuff," she says. "Usually, you're just throwing an instrument overboard. And if something happens to it, that's OK. But you can't mess up when you have a human life that you're deploying and picking up."

NOAA also trained Nicole to be a master diver. Once, when the ship was near Belize in Central America, she got up close and personal with some massive, majestic, entirely loveable whale sharks. "Whale sharks are just awesome," Nicole says. "We saw five or maybe 10 of them underwater. When we were getting out of the water, we were climbing into boats, and the whale sharks were

YOUR HEAD IN THE CLOUDS - FOR PAY !

If you're a Canadian trained to understand the skies, your job forecast is sunny and bright. According to industry experts, Canada is facing a major shortage of meteorologists. ECO Canada, a non-profit organization monitoring the green job market, put together a report on the future of meteorology in the Great White North. The report says more than 9,000 people are working in the meteorological field, but at least 3,000 job vacancies are expected. Why the flood of work? Well, ECO Canada says it's partly because of global warming. "If, as predicted, climate change produces more extreme and variable weather," the report says, "timely and accurate weather forecasts will be critical to reducing loss of life and saving hundreds of millions of dollars for Canadian industry and business."[3]

right at the surface. One of them, its tail hit me. It was just because I was in his way. It wasn't menacing. That was one of the best experiences I've had in my life."

After her two years at sea, Nicole was sent to Hawaii. Stray fishing gear and other debris in the North Pacific can kill or hurt the endangered Hawaiian monk seals. As part of her job, Nicole donned a wet suit and snorkel and removed floating junk from the water. "It was another one of those unique experiences that most people on this Earth don't ever get to see," she says. "Being out there in the middle of the North Pacific collecting debris, where we could see a tangible benefit to what we were doing, was really satisfying."

Nicole's next stop was Washington, D.C., where she spent six months as an assistant to the Admiral of NOAA. (Yes, a very big cheese.) Then, she was whisked away to Florida to start flight training. In no time, it was clear she had the right stuff for a job in the skies. "Once you've mastered the basic skills of

flying, to me it seems like anyone could do it," she says. "In flying, what's going to kill you is the thing that you're not expecting. People screw up, and they do stupid things to get them killed. But hopefully, I won't ever let that happen to me."

These days, Nicole flies all over the United States. NOAA's four Twin Otter airplanes have many important jobs, including tracking marine mammals and responding to emergencies such as oil spills. "But we can also put atmospheric sensors in the plane and do pollution research, which we've done

over Houston and Denver," Nicole says. "We can also put cameras in the plane and use them for remote sensing. We've done coastal surveying in California, and airport surveys in Alaska. We do a pretty wide variety of work." Danger, of course, is the price for having such an incredible job. That was agonizingly clear when Nicole was flying the Twin Otter over the Aleutian Islands near Alaska. "We were flying less than a wing's length off the side of these cliffs," she says. "You have to really be on your game all the time. If you get into trouble out there, the nearest airports for landing are sometimes 350 miles (563 kilometers) away. If you crash, it's going to take a really long time for them to get you help."

"'... if there's an emergency, you have to remain level-headed and cool and deal with the emergency in a logical way. Or you are going to die.'"

Suddenly, the plane's generators broke down. The engines were working, but the flight instruments went dead. With her plane far from any source of help and five people on board, Nicole was living the scariest moment of her career. "It was the most frightening place to have something go wrong," she says. "It was a pretty big deal not having flight instruments. And we were in and out of the clouds. You can get yourself into a really bad situation really fast."

For 20 or 30 terrifying seconds, Nicole worried she would have to ditch the plane in the middle of nowhere. But she didn't panic. She and the other pilot managed to get one of the generators — and the flight instruments — working. They made it to an airport and landed safely. "I think what sets pilots apart

from other people," she says, "is that if there's an emergency, you have to remain level-headed and cool and deal with the emergency in a logical way. Or you are going to die."

Nicole's parents are proud of the way she sets goals and works hard to achieve them — even if that means she has to fly small planes near big cliffs or explore the eye of a hurricane. "We always told Nicole there wasn't anything she couldn't do," says her father, Peter Cabana. "Hands-on experience is the best teacher. Flying through a hurricane is just part of a job someone has to do. The only way to truly understand the event is to do it, and that's what Nicole did. We would expect nothing less from her."

With more than 1,500 hours of flying behind her, Nicole has already had a lifetime's worth of travel, thrills, and adventure. And it's not over yet. Inspired by her unforgettable flight into the eye of Paloma, she is now thinking about training to become a hurricane hunter pilot.

In Lieutenant Nicole Cabana's career, at least, the sky really is the limit.

Chapter 10

CAREER
ACTIVISTS

Revolutionary Rosa

ROSA KOURI, Environmental Activist

When she flew from England to Canada to spend Christmas with her family, Rosa Kouri had no idea she was on the brink of one of the biggest ordeals of her life.

Just after New Year's, the vibrant, globe-trotting 25-year-old graduate student was struck down by a serious, extremely rare back problem. The doctors said she could lose the use of her legs. Trying to save her from paralysis, they rushed her into emergency surgery.

> **❝** ... a lot of people would feel like giving up – or at least taking a breather for a year. But not Rosa Kouri. She was practically born wanting to change the world. And no threat of paralysis was going to destroy her plans. **❞**

Weeks later, Rosa was almost walking normally again. With her combination of youth and determination, she toughed out the pain. And less than two months after her operation, she was on a plane, heading back to one of the most prestigious universities in the world.

"I'm still recovering, very slowly, and will be for months," says Rosa, who is doing a master's degree at the University of Oxford. "It was touch and go on whether I could come back in time to finish my course here. But I managed to just make it, flying almost exactly six weeks from the day I had my surgery. It was a pretty scary experience, but I'm seeing the light at the end of the tunnel."

In the face of that kind of struggle, a lot of people would feel like giving up — or at least taking a breather for a year. But not

Rosa Kouri. She was practically born wanting to change the world. And no threat of paralysis was going to destroy her plans.

Rosa is an environmental activist extraordinaire. When she was doing her first university degree in Montreal (on full scholarship, no less), she started a huge sustainability project on campus. At just 21 years of age, she became national director of Canada's largest environmental youth organization. And most amazingly, the World Conservation Union has recognized her as one of 25 outstanding female leaders fighting climate change across the globe.

So how did a girl from Saskatchewan grow up to be a green hero?

Rosa's fascinating life story began in Mozambique, where she was born in the 1980s. Her parents, both Canadians, were in the African country doing development work. Her father's big project was putting concrete latrines in poor neighborhoods. "My parents have been huge influences for me," Rosa says. "They're very inspiring people. They exposed me to a lot growing up, and kind of helped give me some wisdom as to how to grapple with the world."

The family left Mozambique when Rosa was a baby because of the escalating civil war. She spent most of her childhood back in Canada, in the city of Saskatoon. With activist parents, life was never dull. "I had this family that was always living on the frontier of controversial issues at every era," Rosa says. "And when I was eight or nine years old, my father was working with a blockade in northern Saskatchewan."

THE YOUNG VOICE THAT MOVED THE WORLD

If you think a kid can't change the world, take a look at Severn Cullis-Suzuki. (Yep, her dad is Dr. David Suzuki.) When she was a nine-year-old in Vancouver, she started the Environmental Children's Organization (ECO) at her school. In 1992, she and some friends from ECO raised cash to travel to the United Nations Conference on Environment and Development – it's usually called the Earth Summit – in Rio de Janeiro, Brazil. Severn, who was only 12 at the time, made a powerful, passionate speech to government officials from around the world.[1] "I am afraid to go out in the sun now because of the holes in our ozone," she said. "I am afraid to breathe the air because I don't know what chemicals are in it." Severn grew up to become an environmental activist, author, speaker, and broadcaster.[2] But even after all of these years, the speech she made in Brazil is making an impact: Hundreds of thousands of people have watched the clip on YouTube.[3]

That blockade turned out to be something that would stay in Rosa's memory forever. Native elders from the Canoe Lake Cree Nation were angry that a big forestry company was clear cut logging in the area. For months, they camped on the road in protest. "We went and visited the blockade," Rosa recalls. "And just experiencing that, and being introduced to a clear cut from the perspective of an elder, and having them explain what that means, it was so powerful it was incredible."

Rosa remembers how the elders made a gift of tobacco for the clear cut. She can still hear the songs they sang. But most of all, she remembers elders talking with her, and encouraging her to touch the tree stumps. "As a child, you're kind of this raw bundle of emotions and imagination," Rosa says. "[Each stump] felt like a wound. You touch the tree and you look at this

clear cut around you and what used to be this beautiful forest, and it just doesn't feel right."

As a teenager in the 1990s, Rosa had plenty of pop culture influences. She read about Bono from U2 standing up against injustices around the world. She listened to Nirvana singing about fighting the system. And by the time she was in her early 20s, Rosa was calling herself an environmentalist and writing academic papers about civil wars. "I was trying to make sense of this," she says. "I kept reading about child soldiers, and other things that make your soul quiver. The most horrible things you can imagine are happening in these places."

LEGENDS AND LEAVES

If you ask any young eco-activist to name her big inspirations, chances are she'll mention Rachel Carson. Carson was a writer, scientist, and ecologist who was born in Pennsylvania in 1907. In the 1930s, she was editor-in-chief of publications for the U.S. Fish and Wildlife Service. She became famous in the 1940s for writing *The Edge Of The Sea* and other books about the ocean. After World War II, Carson started warning the public about the long-term effects of pesticides. Her 1962 book, *Silent Spring*, criticized the chemical industry and called for natural methods of controlling pests. Carson died in 1963, but her impact has lasted for decades. As her biographer, Linda Lear, wrote: "Her witness for the beauty and integrity of life continues to inspire new generations to protect the living world and all its creatures."[4]

www.rachelcarson.org

Rosa made a decision. She wanted to do something concrete to make a difference in the world. She knew it wouldn't be right to swagger into other countries, telling people she had all the answers. As a young Canadian woman, she had to speak from her own place, in her own voice. "That's when I started getting involved with campus

sustainability," Rosa says. "If the place that I have the most legitimacy to act is in my own backyard, and there's a lot of ways that my university institution can be transformed in really systemic, fundamental ways, let's get that started."

Rosa launched a campus-wide sustainability study that looked at everything from McGill University's paper recycling to its hiring practices. Then, after graduating with her degree in political science and economics, she was offered a top job with the Sierra Youth Coalition (SYC), the youth branch of Sierra Club Canada. SYC's mission is to fight for a just, sustainable society. "It was unbelievable," says Rosa, who went on to spend two years as the organization's national director. "I still can't even imagine. I was 21. They hired me. And I got there, and there was a quarter-million-dollar budget. There were 20 staff. There were four camps happening across the country, plus a national conference happening. And there I was. I had no management training at all. And it was just completely overwhelming."

But Rosa must have done something right. Because during her time in the job, SYC soared. Rosa was immersed in outreach, education, and youth advocacy across Canada. "To me, Sierra Youth Coalition is just an incredible organization because it's all these incredibly smart, motivated, and savvy people, young people who are very radical in the sense that they believe in tackling problems at the root," she says. "But they have this really interesting command of tactics and of different approaches."

One of those tactics helped Rosa make it into the news around the world. To mark the 25th anniversary of John Lennon's death, she and other activists from Sierra Youth Coalition held a "bed-in for the climate" at the United Nations Climate Change Conference in Montreal. As photographers snapped pictures and journalists scribbled notes, Rosa's team sat on pillows and blankets on the floor, singing and chanting for the planet. "We did some really neat work there," Rosa recalls. "The picture was in *The New York Times*. And we got quotes everywhere."

More than a year later, Rosa found out the World Conservation Union was recognizing her as an outstanding leader on climate change. The honor came as a sweet green surprise. She didn't even know that the SYC board of directors had nominated her. "That, to me, was the biggest compliment," Rosa says, "that the people I work for every day thought enough of me to nominate me."

As satisfying as the work was, Rosa decided to leave the Sierra Youth Coalition and begin some new adventures. She went to Bali for the United Nations Climate Change Conference, later spending a month traveling around

SIZE MATTERS

So how big is your carbon footprint? If you want to find out, there's a way to do it online. A Canadian non-profit group called Zerofootprint has cool carbon footprint calculators for teens. Once your register, the calculators will ask you about the kind of car your family drives, the foods you eat, how much you recycle, and so on. In the end, you'll get a number representing your carbon footprint – and tips on how to be eco-friendly.[5] To find the calculator, go to www.zerofootprint.net and follow the links.

THE SCIENCE OF GREEN

If anyone's responsible for giving Canada's new eco-generation oceans – and forests and skies, for that matter – of inspiration, it's Dr. David Suzuki. The scientist, environmentalist, and broadcaster became a champion for Mother Nature way before green was considered cool. Dr. Suzuki, a geneticist with a PhD in zoology, decided to take his career beyond the lab and onto the airwaves. In the early 1970s, he started writing and hosting a Canadian TV show called "Suzuki on Science." He went on to spend 30 years with a well-known documentary series, "The Nature of Things," and he has made loads of other award-winning programs for big TV networks. These days, the David Suzuki Foundation works to find ways for society to live in balance with nature. (You can even sign up for David Suzuki's Nature Challenge on the foundation's website at www.davidsuzuki.org.) And one of Canada's most eco-friendly new schools was named after this super eco-celeb. Now that's what you call a lifetime of green.[6]

the Indonesian island. ("It was beautiful," she says. "I learned to scuba dive.") Then, so many years after leaving Africa, Rosa and her parents went back to the country where she was born. They spent four months in Mozambique, working with young people and researching ways of bringing electricity to villages.

Rosa's parents describe her as smart, analytical, and effective in carrying out her plans. "What distinguishes Rosa is her spirit," says her mother, Denise Kouri. "She has enormous energy and passion for life, and a commitment — that began at an early age — to social justice and to an ecological ethic. For us, Rosa is an example of the global environmental youth movement that is working to turn the world around to make it sustainable and ecological. We owe a great deal to the fortitude, vision, and leadership of this remarkable movement."

After the beaches of Bali and the scorching heat of Africa, Rosa headed for the stunning spires and rainy skies of England. She is studying toward a master's degree in nature, society, and environmental policy at the University of Oxford. It's the oldest university in the English-speaking world — teaching there started around the year 1096! — and it has graduated more than 40 Nobel laureates and plenty of royalty. "Oh my goodness, it's so challenging here," she says. "It's really exciting. The caliber of intellectual work here is amazing. You feel like you can ask any question, and people take it seriously and they'll discuss it seriously."

Rosa says she's committed to a career that will make her an agent for change. She's fascinated with figuring out what would make people greener consumers. "We need the revolution to be irresistible," she says. "There needs to be momentum for it. We need to make it sexy. I really want to look at that. What are positive incentives that we can use, levers we can pull, that move the tide? ... I think that the world is coming up against its ecological limits, and finding a way to adapt to that responsibly and fairly will be the challenge of our generation."

For now, Rosa's challenges are finishing both her degree and her recovery from her health crisis. A setback like surgery didn't sour her spirit. "I have so much appreciation for basic things now. There are a lot of things I don't take for granted anymore."

And with an already amazing list of accomplishments, Rosa Kouri is walking her way toward greater, greener success.

A Budding Career

Action Hero
ADAM MacISAAC, *Eco-Volunteer*

AGE: 26

TITLE: Volunteer Media Coordinator, Peace Child International (PCI)

THE GROUP: PCI is a huge network of youth-led organizations with members in more than 180 countries. Since getting started in 1981, PCI has consulted with the United Nations on climate change, peace, and other issues.

THE JOB: Every year, the United Nations produces the *Human Development Report*, which tracks things such as global warming, literacy, and life expectancy. As part of his year-long stint with a Peace Child International office in England, Adam helped create a pared-down, youth-friendly version of the report. Adam has attended UN Climate Change Conferences in Poland and Indonesia, and he once worked with a fair-trade coffee collective in the Dominican Republic. He has also been trained to deliver presentations on the Al Gore documentary film, *An Inconvenient Truth*.

EDUCATION: Adam hasn't finished his university degree yet because his environmental activism has kept him so busy. "I hope this displays," he says, "that a passion for the environment can open up a world of opportunities."

GREENSPIRATIONS: Adam grew up in a small community in the Canadian province of Prince Edward Island. "It was very, very rural where I grew up, so you basically spend your childhood in the natural environment, outside playing all the time. After high school, when I started to work on an organic farm, I really took more of an understanding of what a beautiful environment we had and how we should be taking actions to protect it."

EARTH HERO: David Suzuki, Canadian scientist, environmentalist, and documentary maker. "Growing up, watching David Suzuki programs and everything like that, I definitely have a huge respect for the work that he's been doing and just how he's trying to disseminate education to Canadians."

HIS MISSION: "I am trying to show that young people actually do want strong, solid, concrete actions taken on climate change."

Policies of Green

CAROLINE LEE, Resource & Environmental Management Student

When she was 13 years old, Caroline Lee stepped off an airplane in Asia and had one great big environmental jolt.

Until that point, she had spent her life on a street right out of a storybook. With its giant shady trees, elegant 19th-century mansions, and killer view of the sparkling Saint John River, Waterloo Row in the city of Fredericton, New Brunswick, was a picture-perfect paradise on Canada's east coast. Then, her father got a chance to work in Hong Kong, his home country. The family left their little green dreamland and moved to one of the world's biggest, busiest, smog-choked cities.

"It was a huge shock," says Caroline, now a 25-year-old university student living in western Canada. "I really remember one distinct difference was the air quality. You would walk

> **'When you are environmentally-conscious, you are socially-conscious,"** Caroline says, "because you are taking care of your natural environment so as to be able to pass on an Earth to future generations.'**

down the street and the exhaust fumes from the bus would spew out into your face, and you would feel dirty at the end of the day. It would feel like there was dirt in your pores."

Caroline longed for the fresh air and open spaces of her Canadian home. At the same time, she started to realize that Hong Kong, with all of its noise and pollution, was greener than she first thought. "In Hong Kong, there are lots of good things in terms of environment, like density of people," she explains. "And I really started to see that that was an interesting way of living. Everybody living in their own small area, not taking up a lot of space. And I started to become aware that that is something that could be quite good for the environment."

The around-the-world education, combined with a common-sense, no-frills upbringing, helped shape Caroline's attitudes about the environment. Her parents raised her to believe you don't waste things or buy lots of silly junk you don't need. (When other kids were getting five or 10 bucks a week, Caroline's allowance was 25 cents!) Kids at school in Hong Kong considered her "the environmental one." And by the time she moved back to Canada in 11th grade, she was full of passion for the planet. She and a friend even started an environmental club and planted trees all around the school.

After graduation, Caroline's natural choice was to go to university and study environmental science. She did a four-year degree

program at the University of Guelph, where her drive to do something positive for the Earth flourished. "When you are environmentally-conscious, you are socially-conscious," she says, "because you are taking care of your natural environment so as to be able to pass on an Earth to future generations."

The university offered work terms, so Caroline sometimes ditched the classroom and got her hands (and the rest of her body, for that matter) dirty. Her most memorable job was on a bean farm, where she worked on experiments with insecticides and fungicides. "We helped harvest the beans, bagged them, brought them back to the lab, picked through and sorted them, categorized them, did analyses on them, and entered the data into computers," she says. "Yeah, the work was definitely tiring, but oh so fulfilling! It felt like we really put in a full day's work. At the end of the day, I'd shower and the water would run brown into the drain."

On another work term, Caroline moved from beans to bugs. She was a research assistant for biology students who were studying river insects. "I learned the skill of identifying water invertebrates, which I thought was a cool skill to have," she says. "We were able to go out into the field, into the rivers, and catch our own samples, which was fun. We had chest waders, and we were able to wade through the water up to our waist."

The petite Caroline has a huge interest in climate change. She's now in the middle of a master's degree in resource and environmental management at Simon Fraser University

in Vancouver. For her thesis, she's evaluating different international policies designed to curb global warming. Besides that, her passion for the environment has taken her around the world. She was part of the Canadian Youth Delegation (CYD) to the United Nations Climate Change Conference in Poland. "It was an amazing experience, and one of the most insightful two weeks of my life!" she says. "I went with 25 other youth who are motivated, enthusiastic, and very inspiring. Being in CYD inspired me to do more in my daily life. For example, if I have a problem with something, I should not be afraid to write, call, or meet with my politician to tell them how I feel. So I've met with a government person, and been a part of several letter-writing campaigns to voice my opinion about climate policy in Canada."

ee 'And if you really have a desire to help the environment, keep at it.' 99

For Caroline, respect for Mother Nature is a central part of every day. She bicycles everywhere, drinks only fair trade coffee, and looks for locally produced foods. And, like her parents before her, she avoids buying more things than she actually needs. "Girls my age like to shop a lot, and certainly I like that too," she says. "But I don't want to be excessive. So when I buy something, I really want to make sure it's a good purchase. And secondarily, I really want to make sure that it comes from a good place."

Dr. Ron Cunjak, a biology professor at the University of New Brunswick, has known Caroline since she was in high school. "She is one of those rare people that truly and completely follows up on her interest, in this case environmental sustainability

and awareness," he says. "She 'walks the walk.' Her enthusiasm and passion do not seem to have been dulled by the bureaucratic hurdles thrown in front of her. She is an impressive individual. I admire and respect her."

So what's Caroline's advice to teenagers contemplating green careers? "This is a bit cliché, but I would recommend not to stray the course," she says. "And if you really have a desire to help the environment, keep at it. Keep fueling the passion. If this is what you really enjoy and you want to make a life out of it, then it's important to do that. You have to go and get what you really want."

With less than a year until she finishes her master's degree, Caroline is thinking about working in the field of energy policy, possibly within a government body or think tank. "The environmental field, in terms of jobs, is growing," she says. "So I'm not concerned about not being able to get a job. It's just a matter of finding one that I like. I am going to see what opportunities come up. The world is my oyster!"

GETTING THINK TANKED

What's a think tank, you ask? (OK, maybe you didn't ask, but I'll explain anyway.) A think tank is an organization that brings people together to do research and, in some cases, advocate for change in the world. Environmental think tanks are popping up all over the planet these days. To list some examples, there's the World Resources Institute in Washington, D.C. (www.wri.org), the Pembina Institute in Canada (www.pembina.org), and the International Water Management Institute in Sri Lanka (www.iwmi.cgiar.org).

A Budding Career

Degrees of Climate Change

GENEVIEVE GILBERT, *Climate Change Adaptation Graduate Student*

AGE: 24

STUDIES: Genevieve is doing a master's degree in climate change adaptation at the University of Ottawa. Her thesis looks at droughts on the Canadian Prairies in the 1930s, how people coped with them, and what they can teach us about dealing with future water shortages.

GREENSPIRATIONS: Genevieve grew up in Toronto. But her family spent summers living in an old one-room schoolhouse in a rural town. "It got us out of the city and into the woods and on nature walks," she says. "It was just beautiful. There were lots of rolling hills and lakes. I've been very privileged that I was able to get out of the city like that. But I know a lot of other children don't. And so when they hear about environmental problems, they might not connect with them as much."

TURNING POINTS: "One of the first moments when I really felt a deep feeling of being overwhelmed by environmental issues was just picking up an ecologist magazine and reading about different crises that didn't seem to be getting better anytime soon and just feeling really upset over it."

ON CLIMATE CHANGE: Genevieve calls global warming the biggest challenge humanity will face. "You look at the science, and it's so devastating," she says. "This issue will undercut any other issue. So if you're looking at poverty, AIDS, or any other issues, climate change will just make all of those so much worse."

THE ECO-GENERATION: "In terms of the youth that I associate with, we do feel that [the environment] is a defining issue because it is our future, and we know that these impacts will be felt in our lifetimes,

and so we're preparing ourselves for that. It's going to have a direct impact on everything we know."

GREEN GOALS: Genevieve is interested in starting a career working on climate change policy for the Canadian government. "I think that's where we can make the most change," she says.

SPRINGS OF HOPE: "I think young people have an incredible potential. And that's what I see, and that's what I'm always thrilled at whenever I go and speak to young people and tell them some of things I am engaged in."

ECO-ADVICE: "No matter where you are, there are always things going on in the communities. You just have to seek them out and meet other people who have similar interests and really organize. That's my big suggestion — to organize and meet people and act in your communities, and educate yourself, and educate other people."

IT'S EASY BEING CYBER-GREEN

There are plenty of ways to be green at the computer screen. Social networking sites can help you hook up with eco-minded people around the planet. Facebook, for example, has hundreds of groups devoted to environmental causes. Twitter has a big green population too. If you go to your Twitter home page and run a search on the word "environment," you'll be on your way. We found tweets from the Yale School of Forestry and Environmental Studies, an Australian environmental podcast called "The Environment Show," the *Los Angeles Times* environmental reporters – and loads more!

Chapter II

THE ART
OF BEING GREEN

Glamour Green

JENNIFER CUMMINGS, Eco-Fashion Designer

On a hot November day in Los Angeles, a willowy woman with cinnamon-colored hair and fancy flower tattoos on her shoulders poses for pictures in a park. Dressed in a long gray skirt with a cute row of white-and-blue ruffles billowing up the back, she's the essence of California chic. But Jennifer Cummings is doing a lot more than looking fabulous. The 28-year-old fashion designer is strutting her handmade version of green glam.

> ❝ With her patchwork handbags, A-line skirts, and feminine frilly gowns, Jen is on the cutting edge of one of the latest, hottest trends in fashion: Eco-apparel. ❞

"I used a bunch of scraps of fabric for the ruffles, and then I recycled a waistband from a pair of shorts that I never wore," explains Jen, who moved from Pennsylvania to California to go to fashion design school. "The main body of the skirt is actually some cheap fabric that I already had. My grandmother gave me a bunch of old doilies, so lately I've been trying to be creative with them. So I just used them as little pockets on the skirt."

With her patchwork handbags, A-line skirts, and feminine frilly gowns, Jen is on the cutting edge of one of the latest, hottest trends in fashion: Eco-apparel. Dressing green used to mean baggy hemp T-shirts, macramé chokers, and Birkenstocks. But with so many designers now working with recycled fabrics and dreamy organic cottons and silks, you can help Mother Earth *and* look like one hot mama at the same time.

"I think eco-fashion is anywhere you are being conscious of the environment, protecting it, and healing it," Jen says. "Because it's the three Rs: reduce, reuse, and recycle. It's the same thing in the production of clothing. We have so much stuff on this Earth. Start taking this stuff we already have and be creative with it, instead of just creating more. As far as using organic fabrics or anything that's not treated with pesticides, it's just better for the environment. That's just how I feel about it."

❝'... I just really feel that if somebody gets out there and designs something cool, people will buy it. Eco-wear is all the rage here in California.'❞

The seeds of Jen's green dream career were planted when her mom gave her a sewing machine as a high school graduation present. In those days, Jen loved hanging out at Phish concerts and hippie-style music festivals back on the east coast. "There were a lot of vendors and people who were peddling their handmade goods, and it was made up of a lot of patchwork clothing," she recalls. "I really fell in love with the whole scene. So when I got my own sewing machine, I started making things myself. Everything was completely self-taught."

Jen eventually entered an interior design college program, but it wasn't long before the full-of-life fashionista figured out where she really belonged. "I found myself many times ditching out on my interior design homework to make clothes," she admits. "I didn't feel like doing my interior design homework. I just wanted to make a dress. Usually it was recycled goods. I would use scraps of fabric from other projects. I didn't even realize how environmentally friendly I was being at the

time. It was just part of my creative expression. And by and by, I started becoming really conscious of the environment."

Jen had a fantasy of living in sunny, happy California, so she decided to go to Los Angeles and enroll in a two-year program at the Fashion Institute of Design and Merchandising (FIDM). Once she started learning more about organic fabrics, she knew she had to go all out and become an eco-designer. "I was just really interested in it," Jen says. "I loved it. I was like, 'Why not?' I mean, it's so much better for us. And I just really feel that if somebody gets out there and designs something cool, people will buy it. Eco-wear is all the rage here in California."

ITSY-BITSY, TEENY-WEENY, TOTALLY ORGANIC BIKINI

Who knew green could be this hot? Designer Jenny Hwa makes Earth-friendly bikinis out of organic cotton and low-impact dyes. Her Loyale line of eco-chic apparel also includes everything from jumpsuits to dresses.[1] Hwa's delicious duds are getting lots of attention from superstars of style. Supermodel Gisele Bundchen posed for *Vogue* magazine in an aqua-blue string bikini from the Loyale collection.[2] www.loyaleclothing.com

During her second year at FIDM, it was time for Jen to do an internship in the fashion industry. She decided to send an application to Deborah Lindquist, her idol and one of L.A.'s most successful environmentally-conscious designers. Jen didn't expect a reply. After all, Deborah is practically a rock star in eco-fashion, celebrated for her ability to transform vintage and organic fabrics into luscious cashmere sweaters, lacy wedding gowns, and sexy bustiers. She has even dressed superstars like Gwen Stefani, Hilary Duff, and Paris Hilton.

Then, something amazing happened.

"I was impressed by Jen's design portfolio and also her passion for eco-fashion," Deborah says. "For that reason, I offered her an internship. I understand that the design schools here are not really focusing on ethical production methods or fabrications, so Jen's research has been done on her own. She has a good sense of design and is a pleasure to have in the studio."

But the story gets even better.

"Deborah and I just really have the same kind of taste," Jen says. "We agree on a lot of things, and we really get along well. And then the other day she actually proposed to me to be her assistant. She wanted to hire me on. I'm starting that this week."

Jen loves her new job. She says it feels like doing arts and crafts all day. She and Deborah's other assistants help cut and sew the fabrics and appliqués for new sweaters, gowns, and other garments. "She gives us freedom in picking out colors," Jen says. "And

STYLE, NATURALLY

Still think sustainable style means hemp sacks and sandals? Summer Rayne Oakes is out to change your mind. The American model/activist/businesswoman has literally written the book on eco-fashion. *Style, Naturally: The savvy shopping guide to sustainable fashion and beauty* (Chronicle Books LLC) is a glossy guide to being fashion forward – and green. The nature-loving fashionista features fabulous finds like bracelets made of sustainable blackwood, bags made of recycled tire rubber, and organic cotton frocks. The book is printed on recycled paper with vegetable-based ink – naturally! www.summerrayne.net

she always looks at it and has the final say. And there are definitely times where she wants to change around what we've done. But she's the designer putting her name on it, so if it's not what she's envisioning then she's going to change it. But she's really sweet. It's fun. It's exactly what I want to do."

Jen has big fashion dreams. Her goal is to have her own fashion line, a workshop, and a website. "I don't want to be somebody that's just telling people what to do all the time," she says. "I want to be in there making the clothes, designing them, creating them. It's what keeps me going. It's exciting for me. Ultimately, I would love to be able to open up my own boutique."

Now, as she graduates from school and begins her career, Jen believes eco-design has a big future. She hopes teens with a passion for fashion — and a love for the Earth — will follow in her stylishly green footsteps. "We're the pioneers right now, starting it out," Jen says. "But I think eventually, like 10 years down the line, eco-fashion is going to be huge. I think it just takes the pioneers to get out there and make it happen."

Some revolutions happen one stitch at a time.

PROJECT GREEN PROM

Want to be a green dream queen (or king, for that matter) on prom night? Project Green Prom, an initiative of Teens Turning Green, dishes out tips on how to make an awesome, eco-loving entrance on your night of nights.

For starters, why buy a new gown when you can look fabulous – and save big bucks – wearing a vintage frock? Project Green Prom suggests checking out your local consignment store and giving a gently used dress or tuxedo another spin on the dance floor.

If you really want something new, the site recommends buying a dress made of organic, sustainable materials such as hemp, hemp silk, or organic cotton. And guys, if you rent a tux, Project Green Prom points you toward stores that use environmentally friendly dry cleaning.

Then, of course, there's always the option of buying organic materials and finding a dressmaker to create a chic, custom-fit gown or suit. And for the all-important finishing touches, Project Green Prom recommends purses and jewelry made of eco-friendly materials.[3]

A green prom isn't just about the fashion. To get there, you can use public transit, hire a rickshaw, or rent a hybrid car. Seasonal, organic flowers don't have to be shipped across the country. And you can choose a caterer who uses local, organic products and is equipped to compost. Then there's the option of drinking filtered water instead of the bottled stuff.

You can get all the glitzy details at www.projectgreenprom.com.

Seriously Funny

CAUSTAN DE RIGGS, Entertainer, Entrepreneur, & Activist

Do you have a friend who's the life of the party? You know, the kind of person who's hilarious, busting with talent, and über-cool?

Caustan De Riggs is that kind of person. He can crack you up with his Eddie Murphy impression. He writes and records his own hip-hop tunes. He can dance. He's been doing stand-up comedy for years. And on top of all that, he's a smart, ambitious guy using his talents to fight for social justice and a greener Earth.

> ❝The funny thing about this funny man is that it took a sad story – and a broken dream – to bring him to this place in life.❞

The funny thing about this funny man is that it took a sad story — and a broken dream — to bring him to this place in life.

Let's rewind to when Caustan was in ninth grade in Oakville, a small city on the outskirts of Toronto. He liked public speaking, music, and making people laugh, but his real passion was sports. Track and field. Martial arts. Basketball. He just couldn't get enough. "Any sport I could get on," he says, "I was playing it."

And Caustan was good. Really good. He remembers running the 100 meters, about 328 yards, in under 11 seconds. He was breaking records at his school. Track clubs wanted him. And he was dreaming big. "I really wanted to represent Canada,

ultimately, in the Olympics," he says. "I was really looking forward to that."

But at home, money was tight. Caustan's mom, an immigrant from the Caribbean island of Grenada, was raising three sons on her own. Caustan needed spikes and other shoes for sports, but all he could afford was one pair of cross trainers. "I wore the shoes out completely," says Caustan, who's now 25. "I cut their life in half. And I ended up developing a mild stress fracture in my right foot. I didn't stop, because I didn't want to give up. I didn't want to tell anybody."

> **'My mom was like, "I want you guys to be great men in this world, great black men, and do some great things for your community and take care of the people around you,"' Caustan says. "My mom was just my number-one fan that way.'**

Caustan kept his injury a secret for almost a year. When the pain finally forced him to take a break from running, he could have been bitter. But instead, he chose to look for other things to do. He joined the school drama club and tried improvisation. Before long, he was competing at the Canadian Improv Games. "I found out I was really good at it," he says. "And our team, we did well. We never made it to the finals, but we did well. I met some great people on those teams."

Through improv, Caustan realized he could bring people together by making them laugh. He started looking at life differently, finding humor in everyday things. He even warmed up the congregation at his church with his offbeat takes on Bible passages. Caustan was doing hip-hop freestyle dancing, singing harmonies with friends in the halls

at school, and writing a ton of poetry. "All of these things started to come together," he says.

But things still weren't easy. Racism was a fact of life. But Caustan's mother helped him cope, telling him and his brothers they could achieve anything. "My mom was like, 'I want you guys to be great men in this world, great black men, and do some great things for your community and take care of the people around you,'" Caustan says. "My mom was just my number-one fan that way."

Then, a geography teacher helped Caustan unearth yet another passion. The teacher wanted to do more than talk about soil profiles and landscape features, so he squeezed in an extra unit about social and environmental issues. It opened Caustan's eyes to the troubles in the world. "By grade 10, I had already made up my mind to go to the University of Waterloo and take Environment and Business," he says. "I really wanted to learn more about environmental issues."

Caustan followed through with that plan. Waterloo's Environment and Business program was a perfect fit for a guy who wanted to mix the entrepreneurial with the ecological. He studied things like economics and accounting, but they were blended with courses about human geography and environmental research techniques.

Then, suddenly, a cruel Caribbean storm changed Caustan's life. Hurricane Ivan was one of the worst hurricanes in history.

It ravaged Grenada, snapping palm trees, destroying buildings, smashing fishing boats against the shore, and turning lush green hills to mud. Across the Caribbean, more than 60 people died. People who lived through it said it was apocalyptic.

This was no distant tragedy for Caustan. Although he grew up in Canada, the warmth of the Caribbean always washed over his life. Caustan decided he had to find a way of helping the people of Grenada. "[The hurricane] was too close to home," he says. "I mean, you hear stories about stuff going on in other places in the world, and you genuinely feel for them. But this time, I actually felt more responsible, that I needed to do something about it."

Caustan decided to spend a work term in Grenada. When he stepped off the plane, he found an island still in tatters. Beautiful old coconut trees were nothing but posts. Buildings were falling apart. The people were struggling to start over. "It was a sad sight," he says. "A lot of schools were still being rebuilt. It's an expensive process. And relief money only comes for so long, until the next thing happens."

CARDBOARD ART

Now here's a guy who really thinks outside the box. And inside the box, and all around the box, for that matter. Mark Langan of Brunswick Hills, Ohio, takes humble corrugated cardboard and turns it into fabulous, eco-friendly works of art.[4] By making a strong statement about the importance of recycling, his masterpieces salute Mother Nature. And oh yes, each one-of-a-kind cardboard sculpture looks awesome too!

www.langanart.com

Caustan stayed in the tiny nation for 11 weeks, working in the country's International Trade Department. But from the day he

arrived, he had another goal. He was determined to come up with a plan to create a better, greener future for Grenada. Precious beach sand was being mined for construction projects, there was no recycling plant on the island, and the green movement was still young. "These environmental issues were real, and they were affecting everybody," he says. "It's a lush tropical paradise, and I wanted people to think, 'How can we get any greener?'"

Caustan started by listening to as many Grenadians as possible. And that included top-level politicians. "I had to be very persistent because they were very busy people," he recalls. "They were still able to sit down with me and talk to me. I talked to the leaders of the business community. I talked to people in the Chamber of Commerce. I talked to teachers and students and people on the street. I wanted to get a real holistic view of how bad it really was."

People in power in Grenada heard what Caustan was doing. And one morning, his phone rang at seven o'clock, jolting him out of his sleep. "I rolled out of bed," he recalls. "I'm like, 'Hello.' He's like, 'This is Prime Minister Keith Mitchell.' He actually took time to call me personally to tell me he wanted to see what I was doing before I went back to Canada. It's just, like, 'Wow,' right?"

Caustan wrote down his green ideas, put on a tie, and went to the prime minister's office. After an hour-long meeting, Keith Mitchell promised his support. "He said, 'If you can do this, I

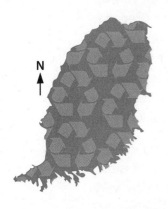

N
↑

will give you rights to come down here and execute some of the programming under the strategy,'" Caustan explains.

Caustan summed up his strategy in a 19-page report called "Greener Grenada." In it, he said education was key to promoting sustainable development in Grenada. He wanted schools to offer environmental studies courses to kids. He also suggested holding a yearly environmental summit for high school students and giving young people information about green careers. "My goal was to help create a culture for sustainable development and entrepreneurship," he says, "where the money doesn't flee the Caribbean and go to some other part of the world."

Some reports collect dust or hit the shredder. Caustan's didn't. And four years after Hurricane Ivan, he was back in Grenada, this time as chair of the island's first-ever International Conference on Green Entrepreneurship. The two-day event was designed to inspire bright young minds. Business leaders, teachers, and 100 top students from around the island were there. So were several Canadian university students and profs.

"It was really a once-in-a-lifetime opportunity for me," Caustan says. "There's not too many students I can imagine who would be fortunate enough to have permission from a foreign prime minister to go back and do programming with the support of the government."

These days, Caustan is thinking about taking his green career conference to other countries. He's working on a hip-hop album filled with positive messages about helping your neighbor and fighting social injustice. He's even part of a public speaking tour of the United States to educate youth about the plight of people in the war-torn Darfur region.

When Caustan graduated from his environmental studies program, he made the Dean's list and was chosen valedictorian. His mother, the person who had always inspired him the most, was there to hear his speech. "Of course, I felt very proud," says Salome De Riggs, who often worked 12-hour nursing shifts six days a week to support her family. "We're not rich folks, but he tried his best. And I just keep telling him to try to accomplish as much as he possibly can."

As he stood at the podium in front of hundreds of graduates, parents, and professors, Caustan kept his mother in sight. He loved seeing her smile as he spoke. It felt good showing her he had taken his education seriously. He even quoted her in the valedictory. "There is nothing you are incapable of," he told the crowd. "I repeat: There is nothing you are incapable of."

As a hip-hop artist, comedian, entrepreneur, valedictorian, dancer, world traveler, motivational speaker, and green activist, Caustan De Riggs proves how true his mother's words were.

And that's no joke.

COOL GREEN CAMPUSES

With so many young people feeling passionate about all things environmental, universities are under big pressure to go green. Not just by offering environment-related courses and programs, but by taking steps to be more Earth-friendly. So which schools are the greenest in the world? It turns out there are plenty of cool campuses in the running. Here, in no particular order, are 10 that caught our eye[5]:

College of the Atlantic
Bar Harbor, Maine, USA
www.coa.edu

University of Glasgow
Glasgow, Scotland
www.gla.ac.uk

Middlebury College
Middlebury, Vermont, USA
www.middlebury.edu

EARTH University
Guacimo, Limon, Costa Rica
www.earth.ac.cr

University of Northern British Columbia
Prince George, British Columbia, Canada
www.unbc.ca

Harvard University
Cambridge, Massachusetts, USA
www.greencampus.harvard.edu

Nottingham Trent University
Nottingham, UK
www.ntu.ac.uk

Green Mountain College
Poultney, Vermont, USA
www.greenmtn.edu

Leeds University
Leeds, United Kingdom
www.leeds.ac.uk

Georgia Institute of Technology
Atlanta, Georgia, USA
www.gatech.edu

In the Key of Green

SOYEON LEE, Classical Pianist

On one of the biggest nights of her life, Soyeon Lee decided to wear the trashiest dress you can possibly imagine. And yes, there is a juicy story here. A shiny, purple, grape-flavored story, in fact, with a big splash of green.

Soyeon is a rock star of the classical music world. *The New York Times* calls the 29-year-old pianist "gifted" and "sensuous." *The Washington Post* says she has a "stunning command of the keyboard." With her master's degree from the ultra-prestigious Julliard School, CDs in stores, and concert dates all over the planet, the beautiful, willowy Soyeon is living a mega-sized musical dream.

Of course, as any musician knows, no classical fantasy is complete without a performance at Carnegie Hall. The magnificent building in the middle of Manhattan is one of the world's most famous concert halls. You don't get to play Carnegie unless you're good. Over-the-top, off-the-charts, take-your-breath-away good. Like Soyeon Lee.

> ❝ ... the one-of-a-kind dress was made of a most unusual material: Garbage. ❞

And so, on a February night, Soyeon found herself waiting in the wings at Carnegie Hall as a movie star, Darryl Hannah, introduced her. Then, as she walked onto the stage, there were gasps and wide eyes in the audience. Soyeon's long, strapless gown was a shocking, shiny spectacle of little purple-and-brown triangles meticulously stitched together. Long, stiff

205

❝ 'What I am doing as a pianist probably is one of the most eco-friendly of them all because I don't even have amplification," Soyeon points out. "I play on a wooden instrument, completely hand-made. And so I wanted to do something in my field, in my concerts, to maybe bring a little bit of awareness. I thought it would be a really cool, small, and important step to take.' ❞

trains on the sides and back rustled as she moved. The futuristic fashion, so unlike the traditional black velvet dresses Soyeon often wears, was like the skin of a hi-tech salmon.

OK, so where's the trashy part? Well, the one-of-a-kind dress was made of a most unusual material: Garbage. Yes, garbage. Almost 6,000 recycled grape juice pouches, to be exact, all of them hand-sewn to a lining of silk. And there, on one of the greatest stages on Earth, Soyeon solidified her image as both a brilliant musician and a green fashionista. "I thought (the dress) would bring eco-awareness to the classical audience," she explains. "And I thought that it would bring classical music awareness to the eco-audience. I thought it would be a really neat way to tie things together."

Soyeon, who was born in Korea and moved to the United States when she was nine, says she has always been on "the green side of things." As a little girl, she re-used her brown paper lunch bags until they fell apart. She has eaten organic foods for years. And she loathes litter. "If I see something on the street I'll pick it up," says Soyeon, who says the United States is one of the most wasteful countries she has ever seen. "I think that it just makes me feel better as a person. We are all such a big part of nature."

But it was the Live Earth concert in the summer of 2007 that turned this princess of the piano an even brighter shade of green. As she watched artists like Alicia Keys, the Dave Matthews Band, and Bon Jovi rocking out at Giants Stadium, Soyeon started thinking about what more she could do for the planet. "What I am doing as a pianist probably is one of the most eco-friendly of them all because I don't even have amplification," Soyeon points out. "I play on a wooden instrument, completely hand-made. And so I wanted to do something in my field, in my concerts, to maybe bring a little bit of awareness. I thought it would be a really cool, small, and important step to take."

The day after Live Earth, Soyeon had her next flash of inspiration. She was walking at Princeton University, not far from her home in New Jersey, when she noticed garbage cans were overflowing with juice pouches. Kids attending summer camps on campus had thrown them away. "(The cans) were filled to the brim," she says. "There were literally hundreds of juice pouches."

Instead of forgetting the pouches at Princeton, Soyeon got creative. She knew she had a concert coming up at Carnegie Hall, and she decided to find a way of making discarded juice pouches a part of the event. She didn't have to look far for help. Her husband, Tom Szaky, is CEO of TerraCycle Inc. His company takes garbage and turns it into cool new products like plant fertilizers and backpacks. (See his amazing

'The gown was unbelievable," Tom says. "Soyeon wore it with grace and refinement, a context that I am sure waste typically never sees.'

207

success story in Chapter One.) So when Soyeon decided a juice pouch mess could be transformed into a fantastic dress, Tom was ready to help.

In the end, TerraCycle teamed up with an organic tea company, Honest Tea Inc., to support Soyeon's vision for juice pouch chic. Hundreds of school kids across the United States formed brigades and spent six months collecting 6,000 pouches. (Soyeon picked "Goodness Grapeness" flavor because of the pretty purple packaging.) An eco-fashion designer, Nina Valenti, was commissioned to create the juicy couture especially for the concert. "The hardest part was cutting the little pieces," says Soyeon, who remembers spending a weekend slicing juice pouches with a machine. "We all put a lot of work into getting the dress made."

But Soyeon recycled more than just juice pouches for Carnegie Hall. The performance, which she called *Re!nvented*, featured new takes on old pieces of music. Bach's *Chaconne*, written 300 years ago for the violin, was transcribed for piano. So was Ravel's *Valse* for orchestra. Soyeon's point? That music and the environment aren't so very far apart. "I take these pieces that were written hundreds and hundreds of years ago in some cases, and I bring them to life in my own way," she explains. "I'm recreating. I'm taking what's old and giving it new life. Just like what's happening with taking trash and turning it into different products. I hope that more people will see the correlation between these."

After Soyeon's Carnegie Hall coup, music critics from all over the world poured praise on her performance and marveled at her grand, grape-flavored garb. But no one was more impressed than her husband. "The gown was unbelievable," Tom says. "Soyeon wore it with grace and refinement, a context that I am sure waste typically never sees. For me, the performance was deeply moving. Her music is captivating, as was the understanding that she was realizing a dream. As you can imagine, it was deeply emotional."

For the children who collected the thousands of purple juice pouches, hearing about the spectacular dress in the news was a thrill. *The New York Times* devoted a half-page spread to the concert, and more than 20 other publications wrote about it too. The dress was even mentioned on the *Good Morning America* TV show. "I still get hand-written letters from students," Soyeon says. "They are so excited that they were a part of something that I wore at Carnegie Hall. And I think for kids it really makes a difference."

> ❝'I am still a musician, and (the environment) is just a part of my passion," Soyeon says. "It's not like I have turned into a juice pouch pianist. So I had to fight that a little bit.'❞

Of course, it's not always easy being green. Some people accused Soyeon of using the garbage gown as a gimmick to get into the media. Not long after the Carnegie show, one concert producer even asked her not to wear the dress to a performance. "I am still a musician, and (the environment) is just a part of my passion," Soyeon says. "It's not like I have turned into a juice pouch pianist. So I had to fight that a little bit."

209

Despite the criticisms of her fabulous frock, Soyeon is always looking for new ways to expand environmental consciousness through music. Now, her fans can hold her green message in their hands. The funky red, black, and white covers for her latest CD are made of something known as "techno vomit" in the garbage biz. "It's really not a pleasant word, but it's shredded chip bags," she says, "also collected by children and then fused with heat. And it creates a really colorful, spunky, very durable kind of material. It's actually harder than cardboard."

And what about the fate of the famous juice pouch dress? Well, it's hanging in Soyeon's closet. And she already has plans to wear it in the spotlight again. After all, a dress made of recycled trash begs to be re-used.

ECO-STARS!

Plenty of big-time celebs are greening up the red carpet these days. While Leonardo DiCaprio was busy becoming king of the world, he was also setting up his own environmental foundation. Since 1998, the Leonardo DiCaprio Foundation has been fostering awareness of environmental issues.[6] (Check out www.leonardodicaprio.org to learn more.) *Heroes* star Hayden Panettiere speaks for Save the Whales Again and is front-and-center on the campaign's website at www.savethewhalesagain.com. In late 2007, she and other activists made news around the world when they tried to stop fishermen from killing a group of pilot whales in Japan.[7] And Brad Pitt's foundation, Make It Right, is on a mission to build safe, sustainable homes in the hurricane-ravaged Lower 9th Ward of New Orleans.[8] Learn more at makeitrightnola.org.

But while she loves standing up for Mother Earth, Soyeon says her big goal is to have a happy life in music. "This sounds maybe a little bit corny, but honestly, I think music is one of

the most beautiful things that exists," she says. "And that it is our sustenance. With all of the stress and wars and all these terrible things that sometimes overtake our lives, I want people to be able to find even a little minute of peace in my music. That would make my life really meaningful, and I want to keep going to make opportunities for myself to be able to do that."

Sounds like Soyeon Lee will have many years of making incredible music, much of it in the key of green.

Conclusion

Well, weren't they amazing?

I knew you would be impressed with the green workers in this book. They have so many ideas, so much passion. For them, it's not just about making money. It's about making a difference.

Sounds hokey, I guess. But it's true.

As you've seen, you don't have to be an environmental engineer or a botanist to have a green job. Every profession can have at least a hint of green.

Look at me, for example. When I was 18 and starting journalism school, I never dreamed my first book would focus on the environment. But that's the way the world is going. We're all part of the green wave. And it's very, very cool.

There are so many great green success stories out there — I'm still discovering new ones every day — and I could easily find enough fabulous warriors to fill several sequels to this book.

But I'll stop here for now.

And I'll wish you luck, once again, as you become a young adult and find your own ways of changing the world.

Endnotes

Introduction

1 Dr. Mark Seasons, Associate Dean of Undergraduate Studies, University of Waterloo Faculty of Environment, telephone interview with Jennifer Power Scott, November 2007.

Chapter 1

1 Bo Burlingham, "The Coolest Little Start-up in America," *Inc.* Magazine July 1, 2006,
http://www.inc.com/magazine/20060701/coolest-startup.html

2 TerraCycle Inc., Urban Art Pot,"
http://www.terracycle.net/urban_art_pot.htm

3 Statistics Canada, "Waste disposal, by source, by province,"
http://www40.statcan.ca/l01/cst01/envir25a-eng.htm

4 Statistics Canada, "Waste Management Industry: Business and government sectors," *The Daily* (June 23, 2008),
http://www.statcan.gc.ca/daily-quotidien/080623/dq080623a-eng.htm

5 Department for Environment, Food and Rural Affairs, "Key Facts about: Waste and Recycling,"
http://www.defra.gov.uk/environment/statistics/waste/kf/wrkf02.htm

6 United States Environmental Protection Agency, "Municipal Solid Waste Generation, Recycling, and Disposal in the United States: Facts and Figures for 2006,"
http://www.epa.gov/waste/nonhaz/municipal/pubs/msw06.pdf

7 RecycleBank, "The RecycleBank Process,"
http://www.recyclebank.com/how-it-works

8 RecycleBank, "RecycleBank Office Locations,"
http://www.recyclebank.com/contact

9 Global Cool, "Get Involved / Techno Logic,"
http://www.globalcool.org/campaigns/phones

10 The Pew Charitable Trusts, "Pew Finds Clean Energy Economy Generates Significant Job Growth," Press Release, June 10, 2009,
http://www.pewtrusts.org/news_room_detail.aspx?id=53254

Chapter 2

1 Kirsten Haley, "How Do Teenagers Spend Their Days?" Statistics Canada, September 2008,
http://www.statcan.gc.ca/pub/89-630-x/2008001/article/10673-eng.pdf

2 Green Roof Safari, "About Us,"
http://www.greenroofsafari.com/Christine.html

3 Green Roof Safari, "Booking Information,"
http://www.greenroofsafari.com/bookings.html

4 Green Roof Safari, "General Itinerary,"
http://www.greenroofsafari.com/itinerary.html

5 City of Chicago Department of Environment, "About the Rooftop Garden," http://egov.cityofchicago.org/city/webportal/portalContentItemAction.do ?BV_SessionID=@@@@1526025220.1249948388@@@@&BV_EngineID=ccceadehmlmiljmcefecelldffhdfho.0&contentOID=536908578&contenTypeName=COC_EDITORIAL&topChannelName=Dept&blockName=Environment%2FCity+Hall+Rooftop+Garden%2FI+Want+To&context=dept&channelId=0&programId=0&entityName=Environment&deptMainCategoryOID=-536887205

6 New York City Department of Parks & Recreation, "Congrats, 'Green' Graduates! City Celebrates Inaugural Class Of MillionTreesNYC Training Program," Press Release, May 29, 2009, http://www.nycgovparks.org/sub_newsroom/press_releases/press_releases.php?id=20835

7 Brian Wingfield, "America's Greenest Colleges," Forbes.com, May 2, 2008, http://www.forbes.com/2008/05/02/college-harvard-uvm-biz-energy-cx_bw_0502greenu.html

8 barackobamacom, "Barack Obama and Joe Biden: New Energy for America," Fact Sheet, http://www.barackobama.com/pdf/factsheet_energy_speech_080308.pdf

9 Velotaxi, "Stable Basis for Traveling Comfort," Vehicles & Technology tab, http://www.velotaxi.de/php/main.php?id=29&menu=4&lang=en

10 Velotaxi, "Purchase and Cooperation," Sales & Cooperation tab, http://www.velotaxi.de/php/main.php?id=5&lang=en

Chapter 3

1 Tumbleweed Tiny House Company, "Utilities: Basic Answers About Plumbing and Electricity," http://www.tumbleweedhouses.com/faq/utilities/

2 aerieLOFT, "About," http://www.aerieloft.ca/about.html

3 Guinness World Records, "Largest Solar Energy Roof," http://www.guinnessworldrecords.com/records/science_and_technology/strUctures/largest_solar_energy_roof.aspx

4 "World's most powerful wind turbine installed near Emden," *Windblatt* ENERCON Magazine for Wind Energy, Issue 04 (2007): 6 – 7, http://www.enercon.de/www/en/windblatt.nsf/vwAnzeige/66BD14BABA2 2BCA2C12573A7003FA82E/$FILE/WB-0407-en.pdf

5 Grant Trump, President and CEO of Environmental Careers Organization (ECO Canada), telephone interview with Jennifer Power Scott, October 29, 2008.

6 Independence Station, "In Oregon, the race is on to create the World's Greenest Building," Press Release, February 24, 2009, http://www.independencestation.com/news/09/02/24/oregon-race-create-world%E2%80%99s-greenest-building

7 Dr. Arch. David Fisher, "Dynamic Architecture: Rotating Tower," http://www.dynamicarchitecture.net/texts/text_16-10-08/English.pdf

Chapter 5

1 janegoodall.org, "Study Corner – Biography," http://www.janegoodall.org/study-corner-biography

2 charity: water, "Founder's Story," http://www.charitywater.org/about/scotts_story.htm

3 United Nations International Decade for Action Water for Life, "Fact Sheet on Water and Sanitation," http://www.un.org/waterforlifedecade/factsheet.html

4 Statistics Canada, "Overview: Human Activity and the Environment: Annual Statistics; Section 1: Food in Canada, "http://www.statcan.gc.ca/pub/16-201-x/2009000/aftertoc-aprestdm1-eng.htm

Chapter 6

1 Great Ape Trust of Iowa, "Nathan 2000 – 2009: Great Ape Trust Bonobo Nathan Dies of Lymphoma, A 'Silent Killer,'" News Release, May 16, 2009, http://www.greatapetrust.org/media/releases/2009/nr_18a09.php

2 Bonobo Conservation Initiative, "Make Love, Not War," http://www.bonobo.org/whatisabonobo.html

3 Bonobo Conservation Initiative, "What Is The Bonobo Initiative?" http://www.bonobo.org/whatisthebinitiative.html

4 Bonobo Conservation Initiative, "Kokolopori Bonobo Reserve officially established!" http://www.bonobo.org/

5 Colorado Outdoor Adventure Schools, "Outdoor Adventure Education Program," http://www.guideschool.com/

6 Mount Royal College, "Bachelor of Applied Ecotourism and Outdoor Leadership," http://www.mtroyal.ca/programscourses/FacultiesSchoolsCentres/HealthCommunityStudies/Programs/BachelorofAppliedEcotourismandOutdoorLeadership/index.htm

Chapter 7

1 Happy Planet Index, "Costa Rica Tops Happy Planet Index," http://www.happyplanetindex.org/news/archive/news-2.html

2 New Belgium Brewing Company, "Sustainability,"
http://www.newbelgium.com/sustainability

3 New Belgium Brewing Company, "Bike-In Cinema,"
http://www.newbelgium.com/bike-cinema

Chapter 8

1 ECO Canada, "Top 5 Green Careers for 2009", My Career, August 2008,
http://www.mycareermagazine.com/index.php?page=159

2 The Campaign for Safe Cosmetics, "About Us,"
http://www.safecosmetics.org/article.php?list=type&type=34

3 The Campaign for Safe Cosmetics, "Manufacturers: Sign the Compact
for Safe Cosmetics," http://www.safecosmetics.org/article.php?id=322

4 Teens Turning Green, "Lips Against Lead,"
http://www.teensturninggreen.org/about-us/lips-against-lead.html

5 Knowaste, "Facts on Nappy Waste,"
http://www.knowaste.com/facts_on_nappy_waste.php

6 Chris Lawrance, Director, JBP Public Relations, telephone interview
with Jennifer Power Scott, June 1, 2009.

7 Knowaste, "Facts on Nappy Waste,"
http://www.knowaste.com/facts_on_nappy_waste.php

8 O. Naidenko, N. Leiba, R. Sharp, J. Houlihan, "Bottled Water Quality
Investigation, 10 Major Brands, 38 Pollutants," EWG research paper,
October 2008,
http://www.ewg.org/reports/bottledwater

Chapter 9

1 CCGS Amundsen, Canadian Research Icebreaker, "About Us – History,"
http://www.amundsen.ulaval.ca/index.php?url=11110

2 Iceland.org – Icelandic Government's Information & Services, "Energy,"
http://www.iceland.is/economy-and industry/IndustryinIceland/Energy/

3 ECO Canada, "The Future of Meteorological Employment in Canada – More Than 3,000 Practitioners Will Be Needed,"
http://www.eco.ca/portal/mediaroom.aspx?display=10026

Chapter 10

1 Speakers' Spotlight, "Severn Cullis-Suzuki, Environmental Activist,"
http://www.speakers.ca/cullis-suzuki_severn.aspx

2 Ibid.

3 YouTube, "Severn Cullis-Suzuki speaking at UN Earth Summit 1992,"
http://www.youtube.com/watch?v=uZsDliXzyAY

4 Linda Lear, "Rachel Carson's Biography," 1998,
http://www.rachelcarson.org/Biography.aspx

5 Zerofootprint, "Zerofootprint Youth Calculator,"

6 Based on information found in the article, "Dr. David Suzuki, Brief Biography," David Suzuki Foundation,
http://www.davidsuzuki.org/About_us/Dr_David_Suzuki/
http://calc.zerofootprint.net/youth/iearn

Chapter 11

1 Loyale Clothing, "Philosophy,"
http://www.loyaleclothing.com/philosophy.htm

2 Tonne Goodman, "Style Ethics", Vogue magazine, June 2009, p. 68.

3 Project Green Prom, "Green prom queen,"
http://www.projectgreenprom.com/fashion_main.html

4 Mark Langan Art "Mark Langan Artist," http://www.langanart.com/

5 grist.org, "15 Green Colleges and Universities," August 10, 2007,
http://www.grist.org/article/colleges1/, and princetonreview.com, "Green Rating Honor Roll,"
http://www.princetonreview.com/green-honor-roll.aspx

6 Leonardo DiCaprio Foundation, "About Us,"
http://www.leonardodicaprio.org/aboutus/

7 Access Hollywood, "Heroes star Hayden on her dramatic protest," msnbc, November 1, 2007,
http://www.msnbc.msn.com/id/21587718/

8 Make It Right, "History of Make It Right,"
http://www.makeitrightnola.org/mir_SUB.php?section=mir&page=main

Resources

In researching and writing Green Careers, we found some of the hottest schools, companies, and organizations in the eco-biz. We put together this Resources section to share some of those gems with you. Here, you'll find information on green schools, eco-job websites, companies, and organizations featured in this book, and green contests and awards. The section ends with a great section on cool green websites we think you'll love.

Eco-Education

These days, countless colleges and universities around the globe are offering environment-related programs. Here's a taste of what we found:

College of the Atlantic (COA)
http://www.coa.edu
At this small, unique university on the coast of Maine, all students major in Human Ecology, the study of our relationship with the environment.

Georgia Institute of Technology, School of Earth & Atmospheric Sciences
http://www.eas.gatech.edu/
The school prepares students for careers in environmental science, meteorology, oceanography, remote sensing, and other areas.

Lester B. Pearson United World College of the Pacific
http://www.pearsoncollege.ca/
Pearson College in Victoria, British Columbia, offers a two-year pre-university program for 200 exceptional students from around the world. Students are selected "based solely on their personal merit, potential and demonstrated commitment to engage actively in creating a better world."

Loyola University, Center for Environmental Communication
http://www.loyno.edu/lucec/
The program, based in New Orleans, focuses on environment-related journalism, broadcast production, public relations, advertising, photojournalism, and film studies.

Middlebury College, Environmental Studies
http://www.middlebury.edu
In 1965, Middlebury College in Vermont became the first American university or college to offer an environmental studies major to undergraduates. Middlebury has made a commitment to be a carbon-neutral campus by 2016.

Nova Scotia Community College
http://www.nscc.ca/
NSCC offers numerous environmental programs, including Natural Resources Environmental Technology and Energy Sustainability Engineering Technology.

Nottingham Trent University
www.ntu.ac.uk
Nottingham Trent has the distinction of having been named the United Kingdom's most eco-friendly university by People and Planet, a huge student network.

Oxford University Centre for the Environment
http://www.ouce.ox.ac.uk/
Oxford's Centre for the Environment offers degrees from the undergraduate to doctoral levels.

Universidad EARTH
http://www.earth.ac.cr/
With its lush campus in Limon, Costa Rica, EARTH is an international university specializing in agricultural sciences and natural resources. A big focus is placed on sustainable development in the tropics.

University of California, Berkeley Department of Environmental Science, Policy, and Management
http://espm.berkeley.edu/
The department offers a variety of programs, including Conservation and Resource Studies, and Society and the Environment. Graduate students, meanwhile, have access to world-renowned research sites and facilities.

University of Colorado at Boulder, Environmental Studies Program
http://envs.colorado.edu/about/
CU-Boulder offers environment-related undergraduate, master's and doctoral degrees.

University of Waterloo, Faculty of Environment
www.environment.uwaterloo.ca
Waterloo offers a variety of environment-related programs, from Environment and Business to Geography and Aviation.

University of Western Ontario, Environmental Education
http://www.uwo.ca/enviro/
UWO offers undergraduate programs in environmental science and environmental engineering. The university also has a graduate program in environment and sustainability.

The Princeton Review - Green Rating
http://www.princetonreview.com/green.aspx
The Princeton Review's rating system gives colleges and universities points for environment-related policies, practices, and academic programs. Schools making the Green Rating Honor Roll include the College of the Atlantic (COA), Arizona State University, Harvard University, and others.

Green Jobs

For the nitty-gritty on the green job market, be sure to check out these websites. Several of these sites even have environmental job listings.

Environmental Careers Organization (ECO Canada)
www.eco.ca
This website is chockfull of green jobs information for students, workers, teachers, and employers. There's a section to help students choose the right college or university. You can also check out the ECO Job Board, which purports to be Canada's largest environmental job board.

Green Energy Jobs
http://www.greenenergyjobs.com/
This is an international job site for the renewable energy industries. It offers loads of solid, straightforward descriptions of jobs in wind energy, solar power, green buildings, and other areas. There are also listings of university programs.

SustainableBusiness.com
http://www.sustainablebusiness.com/
Find international job listings by clicking on the "Green Dream Jobs" link.

Treehugger
http://jobs.treehugger.com/
Treehugger is a media outlet "dedicated to driving sustainability mainstream." You can find Treehugger's green job listings on this site. Most positions are in the United States.

United States Environmental Protection Agency (EPA), High School Page
http://www.epa.gov/highschool/
The EPA created this page as a resource for teens. There's a good section on environmental education and job opportunities. You can also find information about everything from endangered species to sun protection.

WorkCabin
http://workcabin.ca/
WorkCabin calls itself "Canada's outpost for environmental jobs." You will find job listings, as well as tips on achieving career success.

Yahoo! Green

http://green.yahoo.com/

This site is packed with information on everything from fuel-efficient cars, endangered gorillas, and everything in between. Follow the links to info about green jobs.

Contests & Awards

If you're green, you just may be eligible to win an award for your good deeds. Here are a few sites to get you started:

North American Association for Environmental Education (NAAEE)

http://eelink.net/

This site has great information about awards and grants for youth. Go to the homepage and click on "K - 12 Students."

Action For Nature Eco-Hero Awards

http://www.actionfornature.org/eco-hero/

These awards honor kids and teens for creative environmental projects. People aged eight - 16 from all over the world can apply.

The Gloria Barron Prize for Young Heroes

http://www.barronprize.org/

This award honors young people who are doing great things for people and the planet. There are 10 winners (aged eight to 18) across the U.S. and Canada each year, and many of them are chosen because of their environmental work. The prize is worth US$2,500.

Go Green Challenge
http://www.tdcanadatrust.com/gogreen/
Each year, the TD Bank doles out CAN$100,000 in prize money to Canadian university students with green, innovative ideas. As part of the application, students have to write an essay outlining their plans to help urban communities coexist with nature.

President's Environmental Youth Awards
http://epa.gov/enviroed/peya/index.html
The awards, which are sponsored by the Environmental Protection Agency (EPA), recognize American youths who are committed to the environment.

Cool Green Websites

Action For Nature
http://www.actionfornature.org/
The site encourages young people around the world to nurture and protect the environment.

Best Green Blogs
http://www.bestgreenblogs.com/
Best Green Blogs calls itself the web's largest directory of green and sustainable themed weblogs. You can find blogs on everything from fashion to vegetarianism.

David Suzuki Foundation

http://www.davidsuzuki.org/

Started by one of the world's most famous and respected environmentalists, the Foundation works to find ways for society to live in balance with nature.

Earth Day

http://www.earthday.net/

The official Earth Day website has tons of information, including a page on greening your school.

Grist

http://www.grist.org/

This site, which calls itself "a beacon in the smog," is a great source of news about environmental issues.

Mark Langan Art

http://www.langanart.com/

Mark is an Ohio artist who works strictly with reclaimed material. He's getting lots of attention for sculptures made with corrugated boxes and non-toxic glue.

National Geographic

http://environment.nationalgeographic.com/

This site has environment news, tips on living green, and contests.

Planet Connect

http://www.planet-connect.org/

A component of Classroom Earth, Planet Connect is a site for teens who care about the environment. There are tips on how to be greener, articles about climate change, and great information about environmental college and university programs.

Teens Turning Green

http://www.teensturninggreen.org/

Teens Turning Green is an American movement of teens working for a greener environment.

The Freecycle Network

http://www.freecycle.org/

The Freecycle Network, with more than six-million members around the world, is all about keeping good stuff out of landfills. Once you sign up — and that's free — you can exchange books, clothes, or anything else with people in your town or city.

thegreenpages.ca

http://thegreenpages.ca/

This is a Canadian site where eco-organizations and community groups can voice opinions, share information, and make connections.

Companies & Organizations

Want to know more about some of the companies and organizations featured in *Green Careers*? Here's how to find them - and a few others too - online:

ORGANIZATIONS

Aga Khan Foundation

http://www.akdn.org/akf (American site)
http://www.akfc.ca/ (Canadian site)

The Aga Khan Foundation is a private, non-profit organization working toward sustainable solutions to long-term problems of poverty, hunger, illiteracy, and disease around the world.

Environmental Working Group (EWG)

http://www.ewg.org/

EWG is a Washington-based non-profit organization set up to protect public health and the environment. Resources on the site include "Skin Deep" and the *Shoppers' Guide to Pesticides in Produce*.

Great Ape Trust of Iowa

http://www.greatapetrust.com/

Great Ape Trust is an international center studying the intelligence of great apes.

Green For All

http://www.greenforall.org/

Green For All is an American organization at the forefront of the green-collar jobs movement. The organization's mission is to lift people out of poverty through the power of eco-employment.

Humane Society of the United States

http://www.hsus.org/

The largest animal protection organization in the United States.

National Oceanic and Atmospheric Administration (NOAA)

http://www.noaa.gov/

NOAA is a scientific organization that provides daily weather forecasts, severe storm warnings, coastal restoration, and other important services to the American public.

Peace Child International (PCI)

http://www.peacechild.org/

The mission of this non-governmental organization is to empower young people. It supports eco-gardens, children's libraries, tree planting, and countless other projects around the world.

The Jane Goodall Institute (JGI)

http://www.janegoodall.org/

One of the world's best-known non-profit organizations, the Jane Goodall Institute works to make a difference for great apes and all living things.

Roots & Shoots

http://www.rootsandshoots.org/

A program of the Jane Goodall Institute, Roots & Shoots is a network of tens of thousands of young people who share a desire to create a better world. Projects include the Roots & Shoots Day of Peace, ReBirth the Earth: Trees for Tomorrow Campaign, and the Roots & Shoots Reusable Bag Campaign.

Ship for World Youth

http://www.iyeo.or.jp/

http://www.swycanada.org/ (Canadian site)

The Government of Japan organizes this unique cultural exchange program for young people from around the world. It's a chance to spend several weeks traveling on a ship, meeting people, and learning about other countries.

Sierra Youth Coalition (SYC)

http://www.syc-cjs.org/

The Sierra Youth Coalition, an organization advocating for a just and sustainable society, is Sierra Club Canada's youth branch.

Whale and Dolphin Conservation Society (WDCS)

http://www.wdcs.org/

WDCS is an international non-profit focused on the conservation and welfare of whales, dolphins, and porpoises.

ECO-COMPANIES

Chicago Botanic Garden

http://www.chicago-botanic.org/

The Garden has 385 acres of display gardens and three native habitats. Besides being an important center for scientific research, it is one of the most visited public gardens in the United States.

Deborah Lindquist

http://www.deborahlindquist.com/

Lindquist is an environmentally conscious fashion designer based in California.

FUN (Friends Uniting for Nature) Camps
http://www.funcamps.ca/
Based in Vancouver, Canada, FUN Camps is an environmental leadership summer camp for kids.

Lake|Flato Architects
http://www.lakeflato.com/
A Texas firm specializing in sustainable design.

Manasc Isaac Architects
http://www.miarch.com/
A Canadian sustainable architecture firm.

RecycleBank
https://www.recyclebank.com/
RecycleBank lets you earn points and get free stuff by recycling.

Rowan Williams Davies & Irwin Inc. (RWDI)
http://www.rwdi.com/
RWDI is a Canadian engineering firm specializing in the science of buildings, structures, and environment.

Siegel & Strain Architects
http://www.siegelstrain.com/
A California-based architectural firm specializing in green design.

TerraCycle, Inc.
http://www.terracycle.net/
TerraCycle makes an array of cool products out of worm poop, old computers, and other waste.

Index

237

Suzuki, David, 180, 229
Szaky, Tom (eco-entrepreneur), 13, 16–21, 207–208

T

Tayna Center for Conservation Biology, 91–92
"techno vomit", 210
Teens For Safe Cosmetics, 151
Teens Turning Green, 196, 230
TerraCycle, Inc., 16–21, 207–208, 234
thegreenpages.ca, 230
think tank, 187
Thuring, Christine, 38
trash. *See* garbage
tree planting, 41
Treehugger, 226
Tuktoyaktuk, 29–30
Tumbleweed Tiny House Company, 60
TV watching statistics, 37
Twitter, 189

U

United Nations Framework Convention on Climate Change, 77, 79
United States Environmental Protection Agency (EPA), 18, 226
Universidad EARTH, 224
University of California, 224
University of Colorado at Boulder, 224
University of Glasgow, 204
University of Northern British Columbia, 204
University of Waterloo, 26, 51–52, 224
University of Western Ontario, 225
Urban Art Pot, 17
urban green
    David Hales, 42–44
    Erica Stolp, 55–57
    Julian Mocine-McQueen, 45–48
    Markese Bryant, 49
    Matt Lee, 50–53
    Tree Sturman, 36–41
    Waddie Long, 54–55
urban planning, 50–53

V

Valenti, Nina (designer), 208
Vanderheyden, Mark, 56
Velotaxi, 52

W

Wal-Mart, 19
Walsh, Andrew (environmental health practitioner), 13, 142–147
waste food, 98
water
    crisis, 96
    quality of bottled, 153
Water Centre (Calgary), 71
Weather Makers, The (Tim Flannery), 135
Web sites
    Action For Nature, 228
    Action for Nature Eco-Hero Awards, 227
    aerieLOFT, 60
    Aga Khan Foundation, 231
    Best Green Blogs, 228
    Bonobo Conservation Initiative (BCI), 110
    CCGS *Amundsen* icebreaker, 163
    charity: water, 94
    Chicago Botanic Garden, 233
    Colorado Outdoor Adventure Guide School (COAGS), 125
    College of the Atlantic (COA), 204, 222
    CU-Boulder environmental studies, 28
    David Suzuki Foundation, 229
    David Suzuki's Nature Challenge, 180
    Deborah Lindquist, 233
    Dynamic Tower, 69
    Earth Day, 229
    EARTH University, 204
    ECO Canada (Environmental Careers Organization), 225
    Environmental Careers Organization (ECO Canada), 225
    Environmental Working Group (EWG), 231
    Environmental Protection Agency (EPA), 226
    The Freecycle Network, 230
    Friends Uniting for Nature (FUN) Camps, 234
    Georgia Institute of Technology, 204, 222
    Global Cool, 21
    The Gloria Barron Prize for Young Heroes, 227
    Go Green Challenge, 228
    Great Ape Trust, 113, 231
    Green Energy Jobs, 226
    Green For All, 231
    Green Mountain College, 204
    Green Roof Safari, 38
    Green Roofs for Healthy Cities, 86
    Grist, 229
    Happy Planet Index, 132